KITES AND WINDSOCKS

KITES AND WINDSOCKS

Jim Rowlands

Illustrations by John Crooks

B.T. Batsford Ltd, London

First published 1992

All rights reserved. No part of this publication may be reproduced, in any form or by any means, without permission from the Publisher.

Typeset by Express Typesetting, West Wickham, Kent
Printed by BPCC Hazells Ltd, Member of BPCC Ltd

Published by B.T. Batsford Ltd
4 Fitzhardinge Street, London W1H 0AH

British Library Cataloguing-in-Publication Data.
A catalogue record for this book is available from the British Library.

ISBN 0 7134 6705 3

Jacket illustration Crown-rigged Rainbow kite

Page 2 Small school of whales

Page 6 The author in his workshop (*Scunthorpe Evening Telegraph*)

Disclaimer

Every effort has been made to ensure that details of kites featured in this book are correct, and will produce both flyable and enjoyable kites. Readers do, however, undertake construction of these designs entirely at their own risk, and neither the author nor the publishers accept any liability for loss due to errors or omissions.

Except where otherwise stated, all kite designs featured are © Jim Rowlands 1990-91.

Conversions from centimetres to inches are not shown on the Tables in this book. For the conversion information see page 24.

Contents

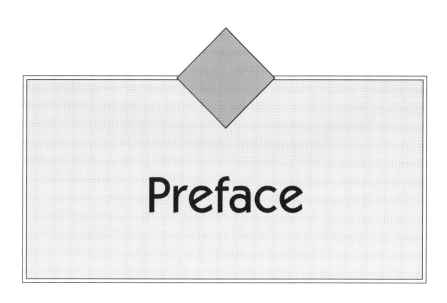

Preface

In recent years there has been a polarization of interest and design effort into, on the one hand, control-line kites: those flown on two or four strings which can be manoeuvred by the flier; and what are described as inflatables: sculpted parafoil derivatives.

Through competition events, precision and sky ballet, control-line kites have had a major impact on the development of kite-flying as a sport, and the contribution of the major designers and performers such as Lee Sedgewick, Ron Reich and the Top of the Line Team cannot be over-emphasized. Through their efforts kiteflying has won a whole new audience, and it is, at last, winning the status it deserves as a modern competitive sport.

Those kitemakers who prefer single-line kites have also been making great strides, and one of the most significant changes in modern design is the recognition of the kite not merely as a lifting device or a toy but as an artistic medium. Its two- and three-dimensional forms attract interest from artists and sculptors, who use it in the same way as they would canvas, wood or metal.

Following this latter theme, *Kites and Windsocks* is my contribution to the development of semi-flexible kites – parafoils, sleds, inflatables and sculpted windsocks – bringing this new direction in kite design and construction to a much wider audience. None of the designs in this book could be described as simple, and all demand more than a modicum of skill and patience to complete. But, as ever, they have all been built, tried and tested in a variety of conditions by me and by a number of my friends and colleagues. Many have also been flown at major kite festivals in Britain, Europe and the USA.

My thanks go to those kitemakers and fliers who have taken time and trouble to assist me in this task, of whom particular thanks must go to Eddie and Ann Megrath who helped test many of the designs; to John Crooks for again producing such quality illustrations; to Winifred Brewer of Hull Central Library and John Harrington of Cranfield Institute of Technology for their help with literature searches; to Steven Sutton for his advice and for permission to publish the Flowform designs in Chapter 6; to Dave Green for re-introducing me to parafoils and teaching me the basic construction techniques; to Paul and Helene Morgan for their encouragement and advice; to Carrington Novare Ltd, Jas Pearsall Ltd, Contender UK Ltd and the British Sailmakers' Association for their technical help. And finally to my colleagues Mike, Chris, Rob, Jan, Liz, Helen and to my wife Ann, who have all endured my manic behaviour over the past two years as the book has progressed.

Jim Rowlands, September 1991

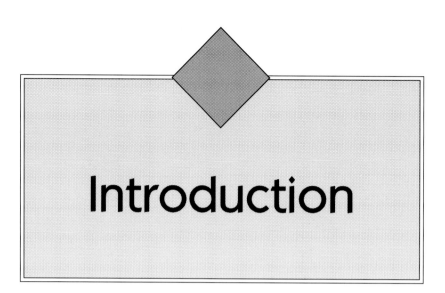

Introduction

Although the techniques of kite design and construction have been slowly changing over the past three thousand years, the greatest advances have come during this century: in fact, during the past few decades.

The aircraft pioneers of the nineteenth century made important contributions to both kite and aircraft design, but by the 1940s their legacy had largely dwindled to a collection of complex designs and ideas, far beyond the comprehension and enjoyment of the hobbyist kiteflier. By this time the role of both kites and kiteflying had also changed, and, no longer of interest to the scientist or engineer, the limited number of designs available were again relegated to the children's toy box.

A new generation of designs did, however, begin to appear in the early 1950s. The sled, as it later became known, consisted of no more than a rectangular sail, with small triangular fins supported by three longitudinally placed spars (Fig 0·1). So simple, it put many of its contemporaries to shame, and has since won many followers. Indeed, the sled has become so popular that it has the undoubted honour of inspiring most newcomers to begin kiteflying.

The next decade saw the arrival of another new genus, although at the time it was not recognized as such. Francis Rogallo's 'Parawing' had formed the basis for many parachute and flexible-wing structures, and the development of this new kite – the delta – was part of its seemingly slow evolution. Two designs, Al Hartig's 'Valkyrie' and Charles Cleveland's 'Glite', led the way in delta-kite design, although many others have since contributed to the process. In contrast with the sled, the delta has a triangular sail, with a central spine, spars to stiffen the leading edges and a cross spar (Fig 0·2).

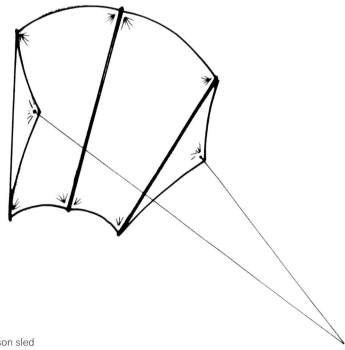

Fig 0·1 Allison sled

The great evolutionary step which distinguished these kites from previous forms was not just their overall shape, but the fact that they were flexible. On traditional kites the sails are held taut in a rigid frame of dowel, bamboo or similar material. With the sled and delta, however, the sails are loose, and use the flow and pressure of the wind to maintain and alter their shape. This reduces the number of rigid elements and simplifies construction without the loss of aerodynamic qualities.

The ultimate in flexible construction, and the design which is set to dominate the kite world over the next decade is, however, the parafoil, introduced by Domina Jalbert in the mid-1960s. The parafoil consists of a flexible 'bag' or canopy which has an aerofoil-shaped cross-section with openings towards the front, allowing air to enter and inflate the whole structure. Like the sled and the delta, its shape is created by the air flow, but it differs from them in that it does not require any rigid support (Fig 0·3).

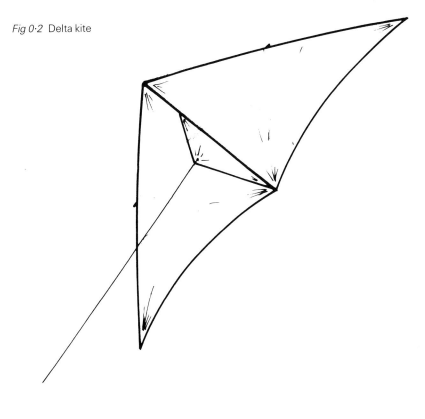

Fig 0·2 Delta kite

ANATOMY OF THE PARAFOIL

Planform

The planform is the plan, or the shape that you see looking vertically downwards on to the kite. Parafoils are most often built with rectangular planforms of 'low-aspect ratio', in which the chord is greater than the span (Fig 0·4a, overleaf), or 'medium-aspect ratio', in which the chord is less than the span (Fig 0·4b). They are, however, rarely built with 'high-aspect ratio', that is, with a span-to-chord ratio greater than six.

Aerofoil Section

The upper and lower surfaces of the kite are separated by a number of evenly spaced, aerofoil-shaped ribs. The actual shape of the ribs has a number of features which play a critical part in determining overall

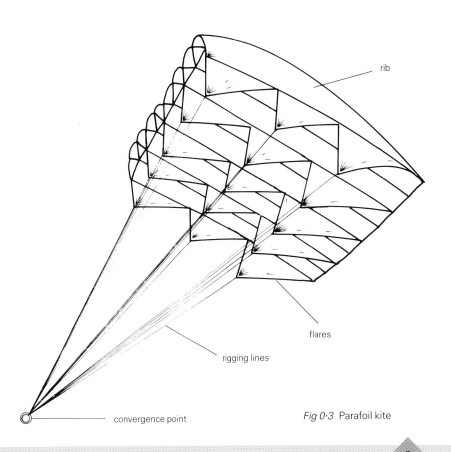

rib

flares

rigging lines

convergence point

Fig 0·3 Parafoil kite

aerodynamic performance. Thin aerofoils tend to have poor lifting qualities, whereas thicker ones are prone to excessive drag. The position of the maximum thickness on the chord and shape towards the trailing edge also influence lift and, more particularly, the range of angles of attack in which the kite is able to fly (Fig 0·5). Even slight changes can make the difference between a kite which flies well, and one which barely lifts off the ground.

The second factor concerning the ribs is their spacing. Like any other structure consisting of a number of tubes, as the kite inflates the pressure on the surfaces causes what was a square or rectangle (Fig 0·6a) to distort and become more circular in form (Fig 0·6b). If the ribs are spaced far apart these distortions will result in large differences between the design shape of the aerofoil and its inflated shape, which in turn may affect performance. Placing them closer together will reduce this effect, but at the expense of increased weight and greater complexity in construction.

Nose Shape

On the basic parafoil the nose is truncated: that is, the curve which you would normally see on the equivalent aircraft section is chopped off at an acute angle (Fig 0·5). This truncation provides the air inlet required for inflation, but it is also the main source of drag. Any improvements to the shape of the nose can therefore have a major influence on overall aerodynamic qualities.

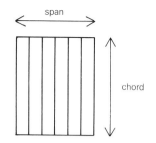

(a) low-aspect ratio

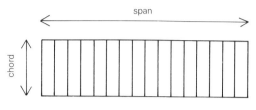

(b) medium-aspect ratio

Fig 0·4 Rectangular planforms

(a) design shape

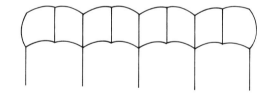

(b) inflated shape

Fig 0·6 Distortion of the sail due to poor rib spacing

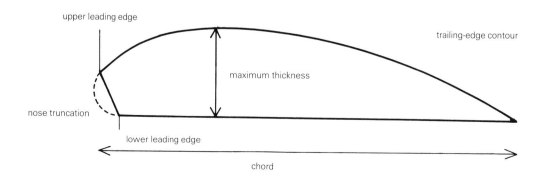

Fig 0·5 Features of a kite aerofoil

Flares

The purpose of the flares is two-fold: to hold the canopy in the correct shape, and to provide an additional means of stability. With regard to stability, flares act in a similar manner to rudders or fins, keeping the kite forward in the direction of the air stream. And, as with other kites, both their size and position are quite critical: either too small or too large, too forward or too aft and the kite will not be stable.

Rigging

Working in conjunction with the flares, the rigging lines serve to hold the kite at the correct angle and to maintain the desired shape. Both flares and rigging lines are usually described by their position on the chord. Those nearest the leading edge are the A lines; those below them are the B lines, and so on (Fig 0·7). The spanwise position can be described numerically, counting either from one side (1, 2, 3, 4, 5, 6) or from the centre (3, 2, 1, 1, 2, 3).

Although this notation is used for both flares and rigging lines, there are actually two methods of rigging a parafoil. In 'crown rigging', lines attached to similar flare positions, the A lines for example, are all the same length, maintaining the wing in an anhedral arc (Fig 0·8a). In 'flat rigging', line lengths vary across the span, allowing the kite to form the flat wing (Fig 0·8b).

Surprising though it may seem, the lengths of rigging lines are also important in determining performance. Flat rigging demands fairly long lines (approximately twice the span of the kite). Anything much shorter than this and the kite will not inflate properly or will oscillate concertina-fashion in changing wind conditions. Crown rigging, on the other hand, can tolerate much shorter lines (less than the span). To be successful, however, the panels on crown-rigged kites must be contoured to take into account the wing curvature.

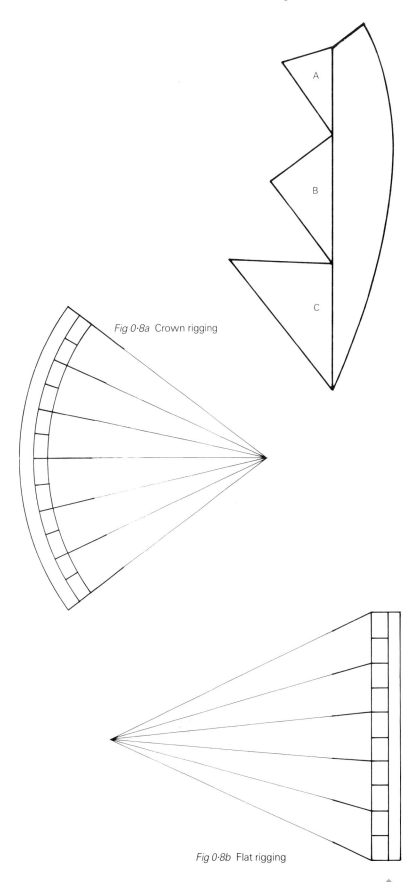

Fig 0·7 Flare notation

Fig 0·8a Crown rigging

Fig 0·8b Flat rigging

Fabrics for Kitemaking

RIP-STOP NYLON

The amazing leaps in design innovation, and the increasing popularity of air sports in recent years can be attributed almost exclusively to developments in textile technology, and in particular to the introduction of strong, lightweight, synthetic fabrics. One such fabric, rip-stop nylon, has been prominent in its contribution to these sports and has found wide application in the manufacture of yacht sails, parachutes, hang gliders, hot-air balloons and, of course, kites.

The term 'rip-stop' does not, as many people believe, apply to the yarn used in its manufacture. You cannot, for example, buy a cone or bobbin of rip-stop thread or yarn, since no such yarn exists; 'rip-stop' refers not to the yarn but to the type of weave.

Fabrics are generally woven from two layers of yarns set at right angles. The warp yarns are drawn along the loom to form the fabric length, and those woven between them are described as the weft, or sometimes filling, yarns, which form the fabric width (Fig 1·1). By altering the pattern of interlacing – that is, threading the weft yarns either over or under individual warp yarns – it is possible to create a number of weave patterns, and some of the names used to describe these, such as herringbone, twill and hopsack, may be familiar.

A rip-stop weave is basically a plain weave, in which weft yarns are woven alternately under and over the warp yarns, with stronger yarns inserted at regular intervals, producing the familiar box-like pattern (Fig 1·2). Rip-stop fabric therefore combines the light weight provided by finer yarns with the strength of thicker ones. Any light tear, breaking the finer yarns, will 'stop' when it encounters a stronger yarn, hence the name. This does not, of course, mean that the fabric will not tear at all: rip-stop nylon can and does tear, sometimes with dramatic effect.

After weaving, the fabric undergoes three processes which determine the final finish and application. It is first dyed to produce

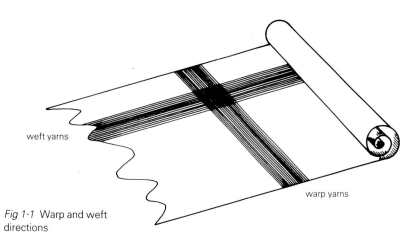

weft yarns

warp yarns

Fig 1·1 Warp and weft directions

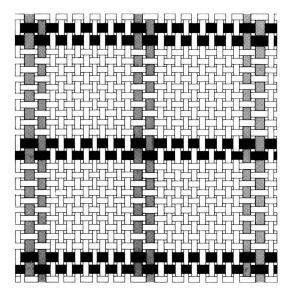

Fig 1·2 Rip-stop weave
pattern

The weight, usually quoted as the uncoated weight, is dependent on two factors: the weight of the yarns, and how tightly they are woven. Yarn weights are measured not, as you might expect, in grams per cubic centimetre but in terms of a peculiar set of units unique to the textile industry. Most European mills use the 'decitex' system, which describes yarns by the weight in grams of a ten-kilometre length.

The weave density is described in terms of the number of yarns per centimetre (or inch) in each direction. Yarns or threads in the weft direction are called 'picks' and those in the warp direction 'ends'. A typical rip-stop purchased straight from the mill, for example, would therefore be labelled: 42 gm/sq metre (final uncoated weight); PU coated (polyurethane coating); 50 decitex (yarn weight); 50 picks x 50 ends per cm (weave density).

Sometimes, particularly with fabrics purchased from North American suppliers, the quoted weight will refer not to a square yard, or square metre, of fabric but to a linear yard based on the standard sailcloth width of 28½ inches (71·25 cm). The difference in actual weight between a 1 oz per yard (ie sailcloth width) fabric and 1 oz per square yard is unlikely to be critical, but, none the less, it can be confusing. A 1 oz per yard sailcloth, is, in fact, equivalent to 1·25 oz per sq yard, which in turn is approximately equivalent to 45 gm per sq metre.

Very little rip-stop fabric is made specifically for kitemaking, and much of that used by both amateur and professional kitemakers is 'seconds' quality. Suppliers such as kite stores choose and sort fabric carefully, and if you are offered 'seconds' the faults will usually be minimal.

the range of colours and then calendered, which involves rolling the fabric under high pressure to flatten the yarns and close up the spaces in between (Fig 1·3). This process gives the surface of the fabric its sheen and also serves to reduce permeability. Finally, it is coated with a thin layer of resin, usually polyurethane or silicon, to reduce permeability further and to 'fix' the yarns.

Rip-stop Grades

Rip-stop nylon is manufactured in numerous textile mills in Britain, Europe, North America and the Far East, and each one offers a different range of weights and grades according to the final application. Sail- and balloon-makers often have very specific fabric requirements, defining yarn strengths, weave and weight. But kitefliers are, on the whole, less demanding and are usually only interested in the fabric's colour, weight and type of coating.

fabric after weaving

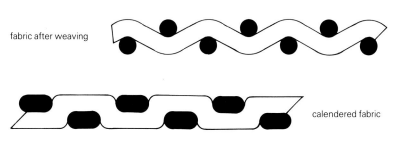

calendered fabric

Fig 1·3 Woven and calendered fabric

Fabric from less reputable suppliers, or bought direct from the mill or broker, should be examined carefully. As a guide, check for coloured threads sewn into the selvedge. These are added at the quality-control stages to indicate a defect.

Rip-stop Faults

There are six types of faults to look out for in rip-stop fabric:

Dyeing faults

Dyeing faults, where the colour has not taken, causing smears across the weft or differing shades along the roll, are quite common and are among the major reasons for fabric being designated 'seconds' quality. Unless accurate colour is crucial to your design, however, such faults can generally be ignored and the whole of the fabric piece used.

Oil marks

Occasionally you will come across oil or solvent stains on the fabric. Fortunately such stains are not usually large and the sail pattern can be fitted to avoid them.

Fig 1·4a Weave pattern on a 'perfect' fabric

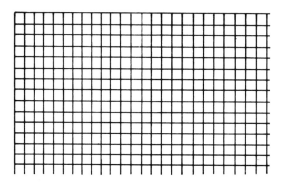

Fig 1·4b Weave pattern on a 'cross-grained' fabric

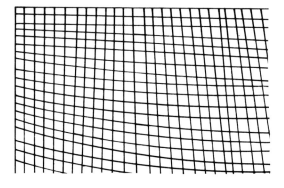

Mis-weaves

You may sometimes encounter 'mis-weaves', or small breaks in the weave pattern resembling a tear. Although often quite small, mis-weaves do create considerable weakness in the fabric and if included as part of a kite sail will inevitably affect performance. Again, try to fit the sail pattern to avoid such areas.

Off-grain effects

Another very common defect to be found in seconds-quality rip-stop concerns the grain, where the weave pattern has become twisted during manufacture. In an ideal fabric, the yarns in both warp and weft directions are parallel and interlace at ninety degrees to produce a regular pattern of squares. However, during the finishing processes – dyeing, calendering or coating – the warm fabric may stretch and buckle, distorting the weave pattern (Fig 1·4). Fabric containing such defects is described as off-grain, skewed or cross-grained.

As will be discussed in more detail later, rip-stop nylon is stronger and less prone to stretching in the direction of the yarns, which in skewed piece of fabric may not be straight or perpendicular to the edge. If, for example, you have made the two wings of a delta from a cross-grained piece of fabric, the stretching on one side will not be balanced by stretching in the same direction on the other. The more the kite is flown the more this difference is likely to affect it, and it will soon become unstable and finally unflyable. Before cutting, take the time to examine fabrics carefully; any skewed pieces should be relegated to the scrap-box for tails, bags and drogues.

Coating problems

Sometimes, especially near roll ends, you may come across areas where the coating has only covered in patches, giving the fabric a mottled appearance. As the coating may still be thin, even in those places where it has covered, probably the best advice is again to scrap the whole piece.

A more serious flaw occurs when the coating has dried too hard, giving the fabric a very noisy, crisp feel. Such rip-stops are quite difficult to handle and awkward to sew, as the fabric pieces have a greater tendency to slide across each other. They will also crease very easily and crack as they are folded, leaving a capillary pattern on the surface.

If there is really no alternative these very crisp fabrics can be used with limited success on framed kites, but they are totally unsuitable for flexible designs. Again, the best place for them is the scrap-box for bags.

Stretch marks

During the latter stages of production the fabric is required to undergo a number of rapid temperature changes (for example, to remove solvents from the coating). Sometimes, as it is cooling, the fabric twists, resulting in stretch marks or a pattern of ripples appearing diagonally across the roll.

Although such marks are quite unsightly on fresh fabric, they will not affect the kite's performance and will disappear after it has been flown a few times.

OTHER FABRICS

Coated and Uncoated Taffetas

Rip-stop nylon is popular amongst kitemakers because it provides the best combination of weight, strength and permeability, but any close-weave, lightweight fabric will actually do a reasonable job.

Plain-weave nylon taffetas are widely available both in coated and uncoated forms at about half the current retail price of rip-stop nylon. They are, however, much heavier, and will stretch much more than standard rip-stop, especially diagonally across the weave. My own experience of buying and using coated taffetas suggests that they can be used with success on designs requiring some flexibility – sleds, deltas, larger parafoils and windsocks – but are unsuitable for framed kites.

NEW FABRICS

With the recent rapid growth in air sports, there has been considerable interest in developing more specialist fabrics for both the sailmaking and hot-air balloon industries. Sailmakers have been demanding stronger, lighter fabrics with low permeability and omni-directional strength. Balloon manufacturers, on the other hand, are less concerned with weight but require fabrics with good flexibility, resistance to sunlight and a high melting point.

Many of the advances in sail fabrics concern the fibres used to make the yarns. As well as many new formulations of nylon, providing increased strength with less weight, fabrics woven from Kevlar yarns are now available. The range of colours is at present quite poor, and prices are high, but it is only a matter of time before Kevlar fabrics are used more widely for kites, especially sports kites.

Rip-stops woven in polyester yarns are also becoming available. Not only is polyester much cheaper than nylon, but fabrics intended for kitemaking can be made to a lower specification than those for yacht sails, reducing costs even further. Some imported fabrics are being sold in Britain, but the quality is way below that of nylon rip stops.

Other ideas are also being introduced to achieve even lower permeability and to improve omni-directional strength. Several interesting fabrics are now available from French manufacturers. Instead of being coated in the usual way, the yarns are impregnated with a formaldehyde resin, achieving good directional strength and zero porosity. These too are becoming popular amongst makers of sports kites.

2

Kite Construction

MARKING OUT

This is the first and possibly the most important stage in kite construction. Not only should the measurements be accurate, but you should also consider how the various pieces will fit together in the final construction.

To mark out the sail, choose a firm, flat surface, as wide as the fabric roll and as long as the longest piece to be measured. An old formica-topped kitchen table is ideal for laying out the fabric for smaller kites, although for larger designs a wooden or tiled floor is much better.

Where the design requires several sail pieces of the same shape and size – aerofoil ribs or flares, for example – it is always worth taking the time to make a paper or cardboard template to mark and cut around. The template will make the task much easier and ensure some degree of uniformity. It can also assist you to use the fabric more efficiently, reducing waste.

Any suitable marking medium can be used, but since kite construction demands a good degree of accuracy, dressmakers' pencils which can be made into a fine point are perhaps better than tailors' chalk, which tends to mark with a broad line. Alternatively you can use a soft pencil or fine-point felt-tipped pen.

CUTTING OUT

When using synthetic fabrics such as rip-stop nylon you have the choice of either cold cutting using scissors, shears or a craft knife, or hot cutting using a heated blade. Cold cutting is adequate for most situations where the edge is to be re-sewn to join it to another piece or reinforced, but hot cutting must be used on all unsupported edges.

Cold cutting

Cold cutting is relatively straightforward. Mark out the shape required and use scissors or a craft knife against a suitable edge to make the cut. The slight advantage with cold cutting (especially using a knife) is that it saves time by allowing the cutting of multiple fabric layers.

Hot cutting

Hot cutting involves using an electrically heated blade to melt and cut through the fabric, sealing the ends of the yarns (Fig 2·1). There are several brands of sail-makers' irons available, specifically designed for cutting synthetic fabrics. Most are easy to handle and their long blades make the cutting of straight edges quite simple, but curves are sometimes difficult.

To overcome this problem many kitemakers, both enthusiasts and professionals, prefer instead to use a narrow-tipped soldering iron. Any medium-sized iron in the 30–60-watt range should be suitable, although in most cases the tip will have to be re-shaped to give the right cut.

For the very best results, achieving a very fine and accurate cut, hot cutting should be carried out with the fabric held flat on a sheet of glass or other ceramic. The hazards involved with this technique, and the possible dangers of working with large sheets of glass, should be obvious and great care must be taken.

Two further safety precautions should also be borne in mind when hot cutting. Firstly, remember that the blade cuts by melting the fabric, a process which also results in some obnoxious fumes. For this reason, ensure that there is adequate ventilation in your workroom before starting the procedure. Secondly, you will find that at the correct cutting temperature the blade will slide over the fabric very easily, in directions other than those you might want. Unless you have a perfectly steady hand, I would therefore recommend that you always use a template or straight edge to guide the blade along the required line.

FABRIC PIECING

More important than the process of cutting is the selection of individual pieces with the correct grain orientation. As described on page 14 with regard to fabric faults, rip-stop nylon is stronger than other fabrics and less prone to stretching in the warp and weft directions (along and across the fabric roll). Diagonally (across the bias) it is much weaker and, depending on the finish, may stretch considerably. If the kite is to retain its shape through the buffeting of the wind, sail pieces should therefore be cut so that the greatest tensions are supported by the strongest orientation of the fabric.

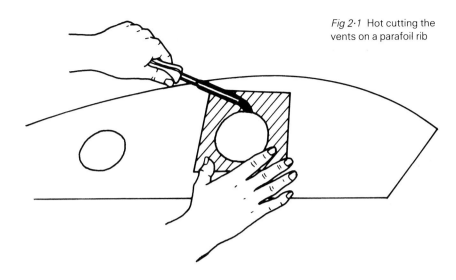

Fig 2·1 Hot cutting the vents on a parafoil rib

This point can best be illustrated with the Malay/Diamond kite. The simplest way to cut out the Malay is as a single piece of fabric with the grain parallel to the spine (Fig 2·2a). But during flight, the maximum tension is experienced not along the spine, nor horizontally across the sail, but around the edges, which in this case are cut diagonally across the weave where the fabric is weakest.

If you were to cut out and make a Malay in this way, the chances are that it would not survive more than a few outings before the edges started to stretch and the whole sail pulled out of shape. Ideally, therefore, the Malay should be cut not as one or even two pieces, but four, each with the grain parallel to the perimeter edge, as shown in Fig 2·2b.

Although a simple kite like the Malay might not perhaps justify such elaborate construction techniques, those kitemakers with experience of winged box kites will be more than aware of the need to consider grain orientation for the reasons outlined above.

MACHINE-SEWING TECHNIQUES

The most basic prerequisite for kitemaking is a good, reliable sewing machine. When choosing a machine, whether new or

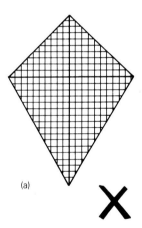

(a)

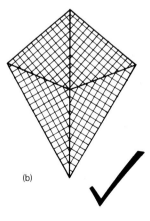

(b)

Fig 2·2 Fabric construction of the Malay/Diamond kite

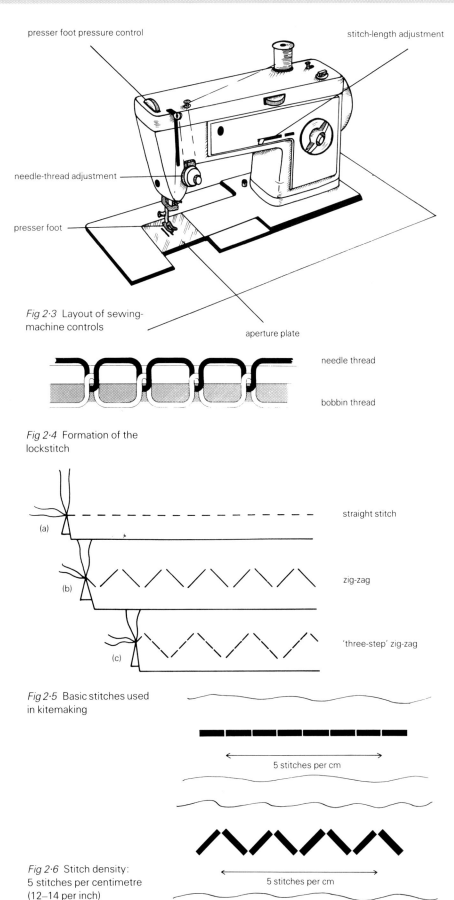

Fig 2·3 Layout of sewing-machine controls

presser foot pressure control

stitch-length adjustment

needle-thread adjustment

presser foot

aperture plate

needle thread

bobbin thread

Fig 2·4 Formation of the lockstitch

straight stitch

(a)

zig-zag

(b)

'three-step' zig-zag

(c)

Fig 2·5 Basic stitches used in kitemaking

5 stitches per cm

5 stitches per cm

Fig 2·6 Stitch density:
5 stitches per centimetre
(12–14 per inch)

second-hand, try not to be over-impressed by the range of embroidery stitches and computer controls on some of the more modern designs, as you are never likely to need them. What you should be looking for is a simple, flat-bed, lock-stitch machine with the facility for straight and zig-zag stitches; anything more will probably be an unnecessary luxury. Whatever the make or design of machine it will have a similar range of controls and be laid out in a broadly similar manner (Fig 2·3).

Stitch type

Domestic sewing machines of the type most often used by kitemakers produce what is called a 'lock stitch': a stitch secured by intertwining the needle and bobbin threads so that they 'lock' between the fabric layers (Fig 2·4). Under the broad heading of lock stitch there are numerous types using single and multiple threads, but kitemaking is unlikely to demand anything more than the basic straight stitch (Fig 2·5a); the single zig-zag (Fig 2·5b); or the 'three-step' zig-zag (Fig 2·5c).

Stitch length

Although rip-stop nylon is extremely strong, perforations such as those created during sewing can create weaknesses, which will tear if the fabric is subject to great tension. The problem is therefore to sew a sufficiently short stitch to hold the fabric layers securely, yet at the same time, not so short as to severely weaken them. A good compromise is a density of 3–6 stitches per centimetre (10–15 per inch) for a straight stitch or single zig-zag (Fig 2·6), although there will of course be occasions when alternative stitches and stitch densities will be required.

Thread tension

A stitch is correctly formed when the needle and bobbin threads cross over between the fabric layers, and only one thread can be seen from either side of the seam. This is only possible when the tensions on both threads are evenly balanced.

Thread tensions should be adjusted in stages. If the threads are crossing on the upper surface of the fabric layers and the stitch is quite loose, increase the bobbin-thread tension. Do this by removing the bobbin case and turning the grub screw to alter the pressure spring retaining the thread (Fig 2·7). If the stitch is tight, causing the fabric to bunch up, loosen the thread tension by turning the dial (usually situated on the left-hand side of the machine). Alternatively, if the threads are crossing on the lower surface of the fabric, increase the needle-thread tension or loosen the bobbin-thread tension until a neat, even stitch is formed (Fig 2·8a–c).

Once the bobbin thread has been set it is usual to leave it alone and, when using different fabrics and thicknesses, make any minor adjustments to the needle-thread tension only.

Sewing-foot pressure

The purpose of the sewing foot is to create pressure between the fabric layers and the feed dog, to control the movement of the fabric and maintain an even stitch length. The pressure required to achieve this will depend on the type of fabric and number of layers being sewn, and you should be prepared to make sample seams and adjust the pressure as necessary. As a general guide, keep the pressure just sufficient to maintain control. To assist movement of the fabric I would also recommend that the standard presser foot is replaced with one with a PTFE-coated base.

Sewing thread

The importance of using the correct thread is something which kitemakers tend to

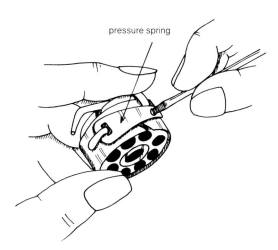

pressure spring

overlook, choosing the most convenient, or, even worse, the cheapest available. But poor thread can end up being a false economy, constantly snagging or breaking, and spoiling the finish.

Like nylon weaving yarns, sewing threads have their own peculiar numbering systems, which to add confusion also vary slightly from country to country. But as a general guide you will find that standard polyester domestic threads with brand names such as Coates, Gutterman or Sylko, and having (UK) ticket numbers in the range 60–100 will be quite suitable. There are of course numerous industrial threads also available and a good supplier will be able to offer advice.

As well as the diameter of the thread the choice of fibre is also fairly crucial. Polyester and terylene threads are the most suitable for sewing rip-stop, as they are fairly strong, resistant to sunlight and do not shrink when wet. Natural fibres such as cotton should be avoided.

There is, however, one exception to this general rule concerning synthetic threads – monofilament (nylon) polyamide, sometimes also called invisible thread. Monofilament nylon is very convenient as it can be used with almost any colour of fabric, saving the time and energy of constantly changing bobbins. However, its smooth surface actually offers little grip, and seams have a great tendency to unravel and pull apart. Except for emergency field repairs, monofilament therefore has little application in kite construction.

Fig 2·7 Bobbin-thread adjustment (reproduced from *The Sewing Machine Handbook* by Peter Lucking)

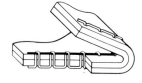

Fig 2·8a Threads crossing on the upper surface: tighten the bobbin-thread tension or loosen the needle-thread tension

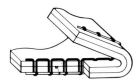

Fig 2·8b Threads crossing on the lower surface: tighten the needle-thread tension or loosen the bobbin-thread tension

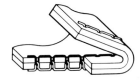

Fig 2·8c A correctly formed stitch with the threads crossing between the fabric layers (reproduced from *The Sewing Machine Handbook* by Peter Lucking)

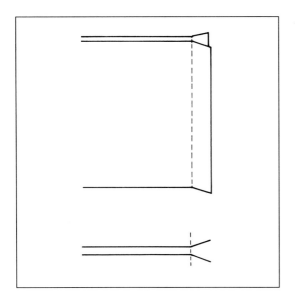

Fig 2·9a (left) Plain seam

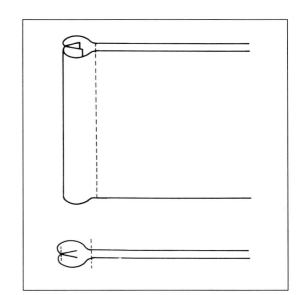

Fig 2·9b (right) French seam

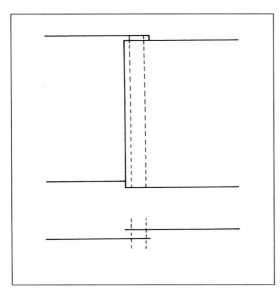

Fig 2·9c (left) Lap or lapped seam

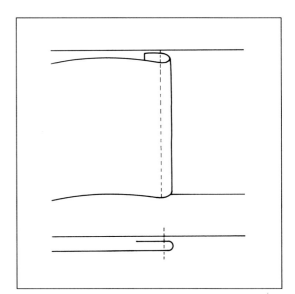

Fig 2·9d (right) Welted or roll-hem seam

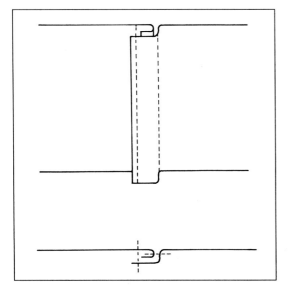

Fig 2·9e (left) Folded or welted seam

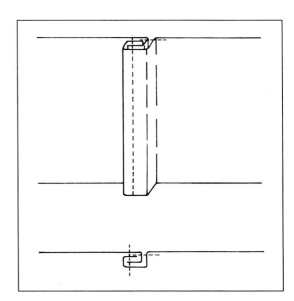

Fig 2·9f (right) Lapped-fell or flat-felled seam

Needles

Machine needles cannot be chosen arbitrarily, and must be selected to match both the thread and fabric being used. Rip-stop nylon is a very light, finely woven fabric and the needle should impose the minimum damage. Too large a needle will create large holes, damaging the yarns and possibly also causing stitches to slip and the seam to pucker; too small a needle may result in snagging and broken threads.

There are two components to needle size. The first is the system number, which determines the suitability of the needle to a particular machine. The second indicates the size of the shaft – either described by the metric diameter (70, 80 or 90 hundredths of a millimetre) or the Singer equivalent (10, 12 or 14). For standard domestic threads with (UK) ticket numbers 60–100, needle sizes 12–16 will probably be the most suitable. When testing a new thread, always try to use the smallest needle that you can, without causing it to snag or miss stitches.

And one last thing concerning needles. Remember that, as on the old-fashioned gramophones, the constant abrasion against seemingly soft fabrics can blunt sewing-machine needles and they should be replaced regularly, perhaps after every half-a-dozen kites. A popping sound as the needle enters the fabric is a sure indication that it needs replacing.

Making a seam

As with threads and needles the terminology used to describe seams can be confusing: the same name is often used to describe very different types of seam, and the same seam given numerous different names. The names given in (Fig 2·9a–f) may not, therefore, be the ones with which you are familiar, but they have been used consistently throughout the book.

To make a seam, firstly ensure that both the needle and bobbin threads have been wound properly. Raise the presser foot and, turning the balance wheel once by hand, allow the needle to enter the mechanism and the two threads to loop around each other. Pull the threads through the aperture plate and lay them flat, to the rear of the presser foot (Fig 2·10).

Position the layers of fabric and lower the presser foot. Make the first stitch by turning the balance wheel manually to ensure that the threads have interlocked, then, pressing lightly on the foot pedal, sew 5 or 6 stitches. Alter the feed mechanism to back-stitch to the start, then stitch forward to complete the seam. This procedure will 'lock' the threads and prevent them unravelling. At the end of the seam a similar procedure is adopted. Sew to the end of the seam, then back-stitch 5 or 6 stitches before cutting the threads.

Edge reinforcing

As described on pages 16–17, fabrics may be hot cut using a heated blade or cold cut with a knife or scissors. Although hot-cut edges will not tolerate too much rough handling before they stretch, further reinforcement is usually unnecessary. Cold-cut edges, on the other hand, must always be either hemmed or bound.

Hemming

Hemming should only really be used where the edge is straight and the grain parallel to the edge. In all other situations binding is recommended.

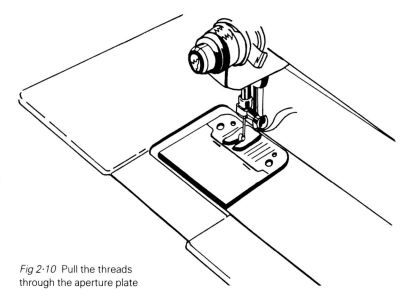

Fig 2·10 Pull the threads through the aperture plate

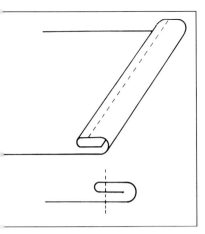

Fig 2·11 Double-fold hem

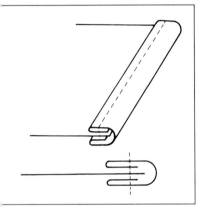

Fig 2·12 Edge binding

To make a hem, fold the edge of the fabric over, perhaps 6 mm (¼ inch), then over again by the same amount. Make creases on these folds approximately 8 cm (3 inches) in length, place the first part of the hem under the sewing foot and continue folding as you sew (Fig 2·11). On softer fabrics it may help to run a glue stick along the edges, or to spray them with adhesive, before folding and sewing.

Binding

Binding is also quite simple. Make a binding tape by cutting a length of rip-stop fabric approximately 3 cm (1¼ inch) wide and at least as long as the edge to be bound. If you are binding a straight edge, cut the tape with the grain parallel to the edge; if binding a curved edge, cut the tape with the grain diagonal to the edge. The slight stretch which cutting diagonally provides will help you to accommodate curves more easily, without the fabric edge puckering or twisting.

Fold and crease the first few centimetres of tape by bringing the outside edges towards the middle, and fit it around the fabric edges under the sewing foot. As you sew, continue folding the binding tape around the fabric edge (Fig 2·12).

Appliqué

Appliqué is more commonly associated with quilts and sweaters, but it can be used on kites to create stunning graphics. There are two basic appliqué techniques. The first

of these is surface appliqué, in which the colours making up the pattern are sewn to the surface of the base layer of fabric; the second is cut-away appliqué, in which the base fabric is cut away after the addition of the colours. With both techniques it is advisable to replace the standard presser foot with the broader embroidery foot.

Surface appliqué

Kitemakers have different approaches to beginning appliqué, depending on whether the design is created as the work is progressed, or prepared and drawn beforehand. I almost always use the latter method and prepare designs carefully and precisely beforehand.

Draw the proposed design, full-size, on a sheet of paper or light card, and paint or mark the colours of the different shapes required. Try to keep the pattern simple, with as few sharp angles as you can. Not only will this make sewing easier, but with the kite perhaps a hundred feet in the sky few people will actually be able to see the finer details of your design. Cut out the paper design, and use the various shapes as patterns from which to cut the coloured patches required (Fig 2·13).

Lay and tape the base fabric on a flat surface, right side upwards. Starting with the paler colours, lightly glue the patches in position, overlapping where necessary (Fig 2·14). Quick-drying, general-purpose, synthetic-rubber adhesives dabbed lightly at points on the surface are quite adequate, but the best adhesive, and one I use in my

Fig 2·13 (right) Make paper templates from which to cut out the various coloured shapes

Fig 2·14 (far right) Glue and sew the shapes to the base fabric

Fig 2·15 (page 23, bottom left) Finished Octagon kite

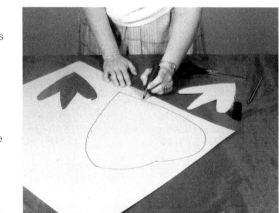

own workshop, is *Photomount*, sprayed over the whole surface of the patch. This dries fairly quickly, but allows time for a few changes of mind. Whichever adhesive you choose, do ensure that there is adequate ventilation.

Finally, sew the pieces to each other and to the base fabric in a small straight stitch (Fig 2·15): 6 stitches per centimetre (15 per inch). For a more dramatic effect use a close zig-zag (satin) stitch.

Cut-away appliqué

There are several marginally different techniques for producing cut-away appliqué. The method given here is one I have used for several years; it is complex and time-consuming, but it does achieve unsurpassable results. The base fabric should be black, or at the very least the darkest of the range being used.

As before, draw the design on a sheet of paper or light card, but this time leave a gap of at least 6 mm (¼ inch) between two adjacent coloured sections (Fig 2·16). Cut away the parts of the design representing the colours to leave an outline, and use this as a template to re-draw the design on the right side of the base fabric (Fig 2·17).

Cut suitably-coloured patches of fabric one at a time and lightly glue them to the base fabric on the wrong (under) side. Sew them in position with two seams of narrow stitches (6 per cm; 15 per inch) following the lines previously drawn. When all the coloured pieces are in position, cut away the base fabric to reveal the pattern (Fig 2·18).

Fig 2·16 Draw the design on card, leaving at least 6 mm (¼ inch) between any two colours

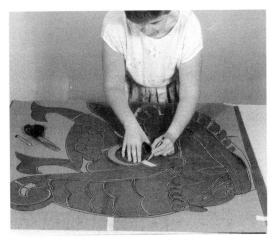

Fig 2·17 Use the template to transfer the design to the right side of the base fabric

Fig 2·18 Sew the coloured shapes to the wrong side of the fabric. Cut away the base fabric to reveal the pattern

3

Kite Projects

As most of the kites featured in this book share the same basic construction method, this chapter describes the technique in broad outline. More specific details are given in the section on each individual kite.

Included with each design are descriptions of the fabric pieces to be cut and their dimensions. In all cases, metric units (centimetres) have been used, and wherever possible these should be followed. If you prefer to work in imperial units, divide the centimetre dimensions by 2·54 to translate them into inches and mark out to the nearest tenth of an inch. Please note that the drawings illustrating each design are not necessarily exactly to scale.

Fabric requirements refer to a standard-width roll of 104 cm (41 inches) and are approximate; weights are measured in grams per square metre (oz per square yard).

CUTTING OUT

The first stage of kite construction is to mark and cut out all the fabric pieces. Begin with the largest pieces, usually the back and front, then move on to the ribs, and finally the flares. Marking out in this order will help to reduce waste. Fig 3·1 illustrates the convention used to represent hot-cut edges, bound edges, sewing lines and so on. Except where otherwise indicated, the back, front and ribs should be cut with the grain parallel to the chord line. On some designs – the frog, for example (see page 67) – a marginal improvement may be achieved by cutting the ribs with the grain at an angle, but *never* cut either the back or front with the grain on the diagonal.

In almost all cases, the aerofoil shape of the ribs is given in the form of a table, indicating the height of the upper surface at regular distances from the leading edge (Fig 3·2). To make the template, draw a horizontal line as long as the indicated chord length. Mark the position of the leading and trailing edges, then use a ruler and set square to mark the positions of the vertical lines.

Mark the appropriate vertical distances indicated in the table, and join them together by drawing a smooth line to describe the shape of the aerofoil. Mark the positions of the vent holes and the nose shaping, as shown in the other illustrations. Use this shape as a template to mark out the required number of ribs. Vent holes are usually cut into all but the two outermost ribs, and if at all possible should be hot cut (see pages 16–17).

The flares should be cut in a slightly different manner, depending on their position on the chord. The distribution of air pressure on the upper and lower surfaces of the kite is such that the line tension is spread out in slightly different directions amongst the flares and rigging lines. Those flares towards the leading edge should be cut with the grain parallel to the forward edge, and those at the trailing edge with the grain parallel to the aft edge (Fig 3·3).

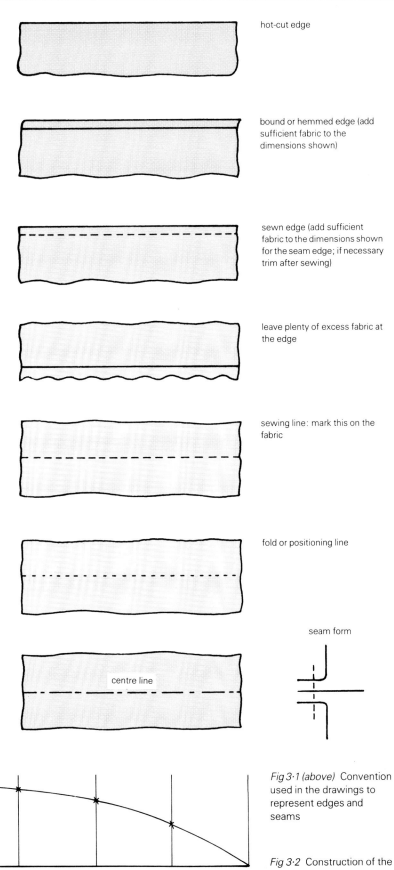

Fig 3·3 Grain orientation of ribs and flares

hot-cut edge

bound or hemmed edge (add sufficient fabric to the dimensions shown)

sewn edge (add sufficient fabric to the dimensions shown for the seam edge; if necessary trim after sewing)

leave plenty of excess fabric at the edge

sewing line: mark this on the fabric

fold or positioning line

seam form

centre line

Fig 3·1 (above) Convention used in the drawings to represent edges and seams

Fig 3·2 Construction of the rib template

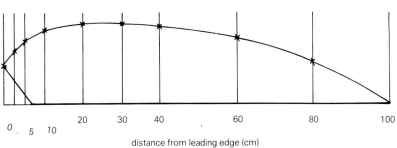

height of upper surface

0 5 10   20   30   40   60   80   100

distance from leading edge (cm)

HEMS AND BINDING

All marked edges should then be bound or hemmed using the methods described on pages 21–2.

SEWING TOGETHER

If the back and front are to be constructed from a number of separate pieces (see the instructions given with each kite) they should now be sewn together. In many of the designs the flares are also sewn within the seams joining front pieces (Fig 3·4).

At this stage it is also useful to sew short tape loops to the flare tips. Even with the largest kites the loops should not require excessive reinforcement, and certainly for all those featured in Chapters 4–8, tapes made from folded strips of scrap rip-stop fabric are sufficient (Fig 3·5). They may be sewn to the flare tip in a variety of seam patterns (Fig 3·6).

RIBS

For most parafoils – that is, those with closed trailing edges – the next stage is to sew the inner ribs to the canopy front. Start the seam from the leading edge and sew towards the trailing edge (Fig 3·7). Sew all the ribs except the outermost ones.

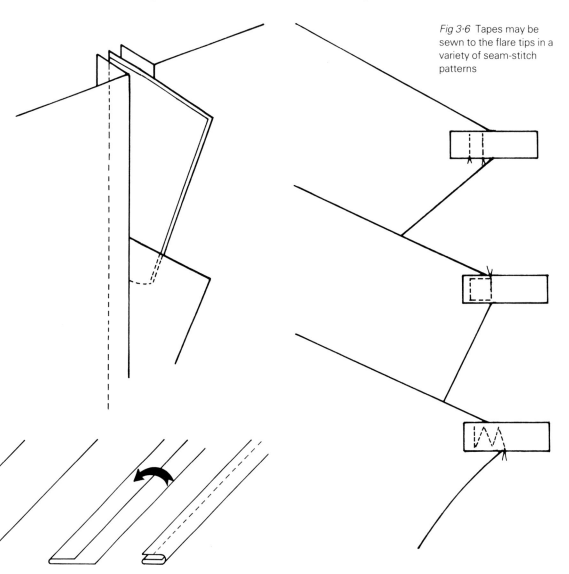

Fig 3·4 On many designs the flares are sandwiched between the sail pieces making up the front of the kite

Fig 3·6 Tapes may be sewn to the flare tips in a variety of seam-stitch patterns

Fig 3·5 Suitable tapes can be made from scrap fabric, cut into strips and folded

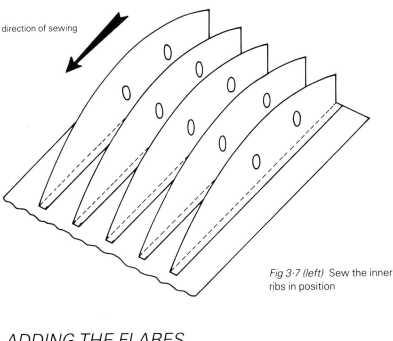

direction of sewing

Fig 3·7 (left) Sew the inner ribs in position

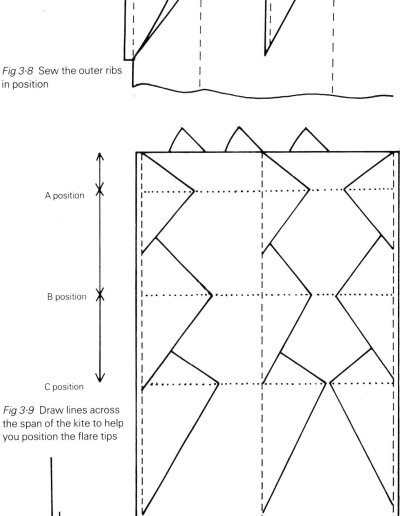

Fig 3·8 Sew the outer ribs in position

A position

B position

C position

Fig 3·9 Draw lines across the span of the kite to help you position the flare tips

ADDING THE FLARES

Flares which are sewn directly to the front of the kite, rather than as a sandwich (see Fig 3·4) are usually added after the ribs. To achieve good stable flight it is important to get the tips of each set of flares in exactly the same point on the chord. To do this you may find it helpful to draw lines across the span to indicate their positions (Fig 3·9). In each case, measurements should be taken from the forward edge of the lower (front) surface, not the trailing edge.

Flares are usually sewn at every other rib postion. Start with the A flare, then overlap the B flare, and C flare and so on, moving next to the adjacent set of flares. To create a neat edge, a welted seam is better than the plain seam (see Fig 2·9d on page 20). In constructing parafoils for myself I also find it helpful to glue the flares in position before sewing.

Finally, add the outermost ribs, sewing to ensure that the seam edge sits on the inside (Fig 3·8).

Fig 3·10a Roll up the kite from one side

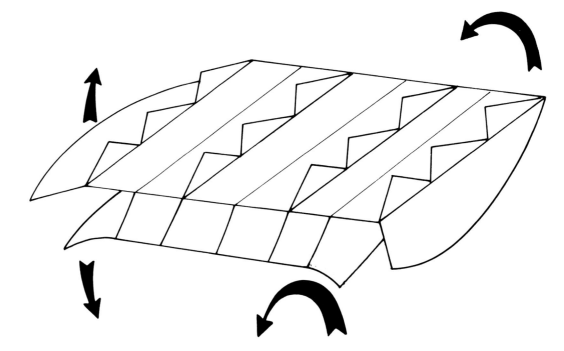

Fig 3·10b Wrap the loose edges of the flare and back around the roll

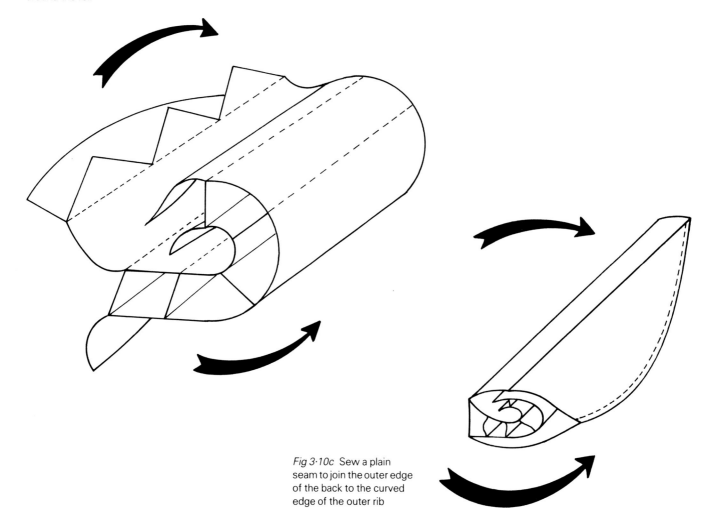

Fig 3·10c Sew a plain seam to join the outer edge of the back to the curved edge of the outer rib

SEWING THE BACK

Sewing the back is usually the most awkward part of making a parafoil, and is where an inexperienced kitemaker is likely to run into most problems. Sew it right and your kite will fly high and stable; sew it wrong, with puckered seams, and it will just dance around the sky like something demented.

Each rib should be sewn completely along the seam from the forward to the trailing edge. Start with the second-to-outermost rib and continue from left to right or from right to left as you wish, or, as I generally prefer, start at the centre ribs and work outwards. As you sew each rib, check at the trailing edge for puckering, stretching and uneven sewing and assure yourself that the upper (front) trailing edge is able to sit flat on the lower (back) one.

The two outer ribs should be sewn last. Roll the kite up from one end, and fold the loose edges of the rib and back to enclose the rest of the kite. Join them together with a plain seam. Turn the roll inside out and repeat this procedure from the other side (Fig 3·10a–c).

CLOSING THE TRAILING EDGE

To close off the trailing edge, there are two options: hemming or binding (see pages 21–2). A double-fold hem is recommended for rectangular parafoils and Flowforms; but for non-rectangular designs it is much easier to bind the trailing edge.

To make the hem, trim off any large excesses of fabric, on both the front and back, leaving perhaps 4 cm (1½ inches). Glue these two edges together. Now fold them twice, folding from front to back, and sew a single line of stitches along the trailing edge to create a clean, neat hem (Fig 3·11).

If you prefer to bind, trim the excess fabric leaving 2–3 cm (1 inch) at the trailing edges, again ensuring that the edge is parallel to the marked line. Lightly glue the edges together and, using a broad tape, bind with a single row of stitches.

RIGGING

As well as being the final stage of kite construction, rigging – the fitting of the numerous lines to the kite – is the most important and indeed the most difficult. The lines not only hold the kite at the correct flying angle, as with framed kites, but also maintain the correct form and shape.

To prevent the collapse of the central cells and spanwise concertina oscillations, the lines on flat-rigged kites need to be fairly long: in the region of twice the span. Such long lengths can, however, cause a slight increase in drag and stability problems due to line stretch, so it is particularly important that rigging lines are chosen with care.

Nylon has very poor stretch resistance and should only be used as a last resort. Braided polyester (when balancing cost against strength and elasticity) is much better, and Dacron better still. The newer braided lines such as Spectra and Dyneema, with suitable sleeving, can also make good rigging lines, although their narrower diameters may increase the tendency to tangle. For safety reasons, I would not recommend the use of Kevlar for either rigging or flying line under any circumstances.

The notation used throughout the rest of the book is as described on page 11. The A lines and flares are positioned nearest the leading edge, next come the B lines and so on towards the trailing edge. Spanwise, flares and lines are described numerically from the centre (3, 2, 1, 1, 2, 3) or (5, 4, 3, 2, 1, 2, 3, 4, 5). The actual technique of rigging can be illustrated with a three-cell kite (Fig 3·12, overleaf).

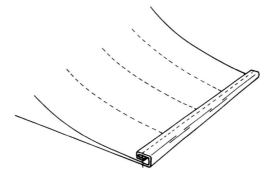

Fig 3·11 Close the trailing edge with a double-fold hem and a single line of stitches

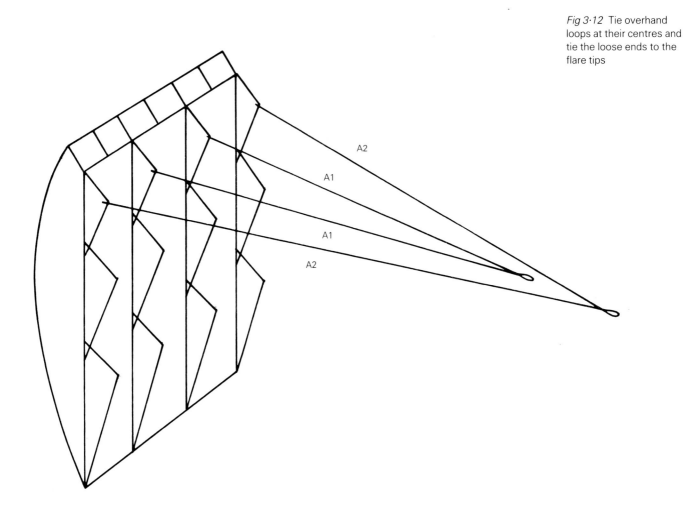

Fig 3·12 Tie overhand loops at their centres and tie the loose ends to the flare tips

A2

A1

A1

A2

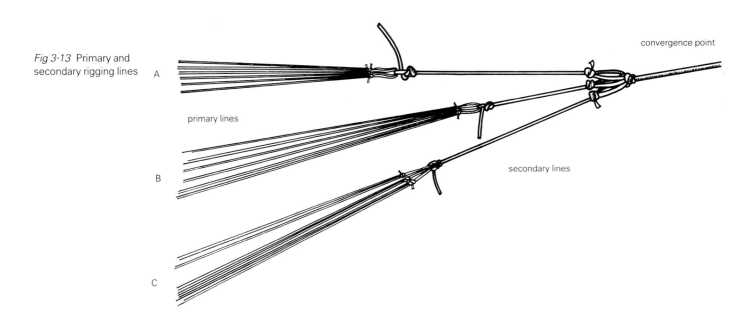

Fig 3·13 Primary and secondary rigging lines

convergence point

primary lines

secondary lines

A

B

C

Fig 3·14 Checking and adjusting lengths of rigging lines

Dimensions of rigging lines for each design are given in the form of a table, and refer to the distance between the flare tips and the convergence point – the points where all the lines meet. Please note that this is not necessarily the point at which the flying line is tied.

To start the procedure cut some line slightly shorter than twice the indicated length for the A2 lines and tie an overhand loop at its centre. Tie the loose ends to the A2 flare tips. Similarly, cut a line just a few centimetres shorter than the dimension indicated for the A1 lines, tie an overhand loop at the centre, and the loose ends at the flare tips. These lines are described as the primary lines.

Thread another short length (20–30 cm; 8–12 inches) of slightly stronger line through the central loops of the primary lines, and tie it off with a suitable knot, such as a half-blood knot. Tie an overhand loop at the loose end. This becomes the secondary line.

Tie similar sets of primary and secondary lines to the B and C flares.

Collect the A, B, and C secondary lines together and tie another short length of line, the tertiary line, through the loops. Tie a loop at the loose end to create a suitable towing point from which to connect the flying line (Fig 3·13).

Peg the towing point to the ground, or to a table if you are indoors, and adjust the lines so that the distance from the convergence point – the point where the secondary lines converge – to the flare tips corresponds to the measurements shown in the table. The secondary lines should be no shorter than 5 per cent and no longer than 10 per cent of the total.

Kitemakers have their own particular techniques for adjusting the rigging lines. I normally check and adjust lines under a slight tension, setting the outermost and innermost to the dimensions required, and the rest by comparing them with their immediate neighbours.

Although when you first rig the kite every line will seem exactly right, some stretching will occur during the first couple of flights and all lines will have to be checked and adjusted again.

Once the rigging lines have been set, some minor adjustments in shortening or lengthening the secondary lines can be done on the field. If you do make such adjustments, remember that if you alter one set of lines to increase or decrease the angle of attack, you must compensate and alter them all accordingly.

Sleds

HYBRID

Derived from Ed Grauel's 'Bullet' sled kite, the Hybrid is a simple kite to make and a good introduction to the techniques of soft-kite construction.

Materials

Fabric: 1·25 metres of 40–60 gm (1½ yds of 1·25 oz) rip-stop nylon
Bridle: 5 metres (5 yds) braided polyester
Flying line: 12 kg (30 lb) polyester

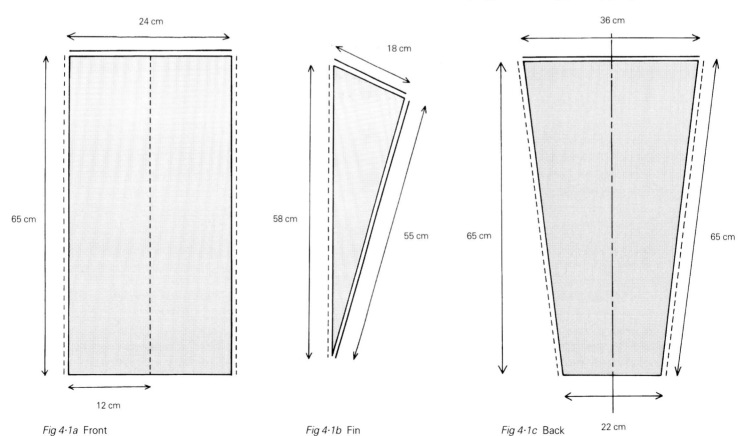

Fig 4·1a Front   *Fig 4·1b* Fin   *Fig 4·1c* Back

Construction

1 Mark and cut out two back pieces, the front and three fins (Fig 4·1a–c).

2 Hem or bind the edges as shown, and sew short tape loops to the fin tips.

3 Sew the two rear 'tube' pieces to the front with a single seam along the centre line. It may help to lightly glue or tape the pieces in position first.

4 Sew the middle fin in position on the opposite side, along the centre seam line (Fig 4·2).

5 Sew the outer fins, points inwards, to each of the front outer edges.

6 To complete the kite, lay it flat (fins upwards) and roll the right-hand side (Fig 4·3) to the central seam, then bring the loose edges of the back piece to the left-hand side to enclose the roll. Sew a plain seam to join the two edges, unfold the kite and repeat on the left-hand side. The final seam pattern is illustrated in Fig 4·4.

7 Add a three-leg bridle, the inner leg 140 cm (55 inches), the outer ones 141 cm (55½ inches) (Fig 4·5).

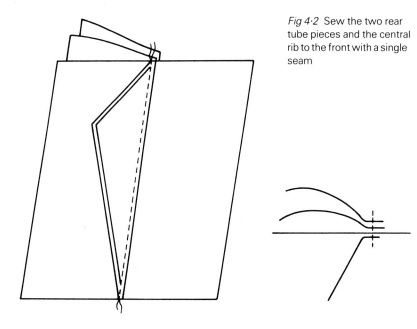

Fig 4·2 Sew the two rear tube pieces and the central rib to the front with a single seam

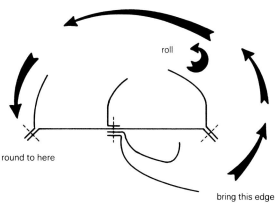

Fig 4·3 Roll the kite from one side and bring the loose edges round to enclose the roll

roll

round to here

bring this edge

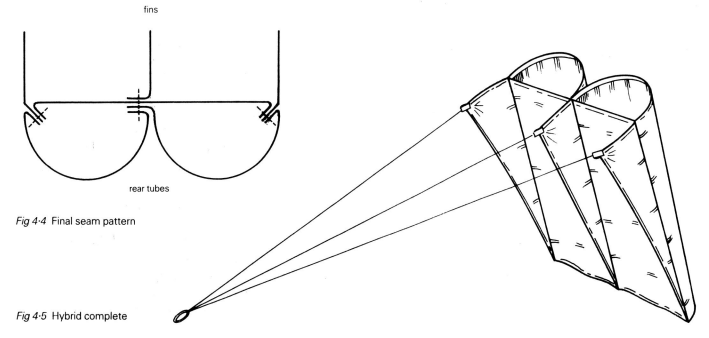

fins

rear tubes

Fig 4·4 Final seam pattern

Fig 4·5 Hybrid complete

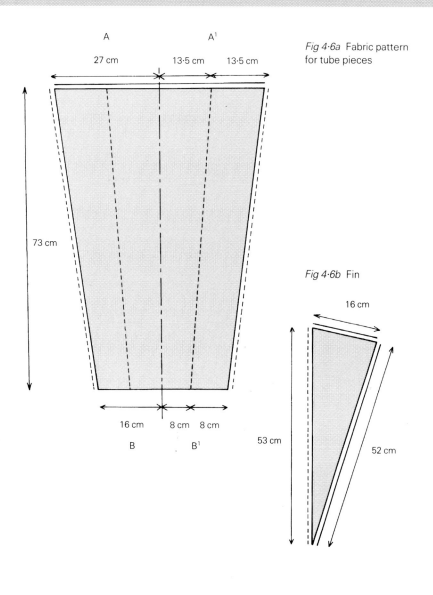

A   A¹

27 cm   13·5 cm   13·5 cm

Fig 4·6a Fabric pattern for tube pieces

73 cm

16 cm   8 cm   8 cm

B   B¹

Fig 4·6b Fin

16 cm

53 cm

52 cm

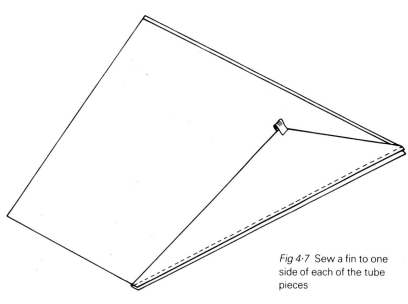

Fig 4·7 Sew a fin to one side of each of the tube pieces

MULTITUBE

An interesting kite in concept; more than a sled, yet not a parafoil. Like the Flowforms featured in Chapter 6 it relies for its stability on the flow of air through the tubes, which are only slightly tapered.

Materials

Fabric: 1·5 metres of 40–60 gm (1¾ yds of 1·25 oz) rip-stop nylon
Rigging lines: 7 metres (8 yds) braided polyester
Flying line: 30 kg (70 lb) polyester

Construction

1 Mark and cut out four tube pieces (Fig 4·6a) and four fins (Fig 4·6b).

2 Bind the edges as shown. Sew short tape loops to the fin tips.

3 Sew a fin, point inwards, to one edge (either all left-hand or all right-hand) of each of the tube pieces (Fig 4·7).

4 Now join the tube pieces, each to its neighbour, with a seam along the marked lines AB (Fig 4·8).

5 To complete the kite, lay it flat and roll it from the left-hand side, then bring the two loose edges on the right-hand side round to enclose the roll, using the technique described for the Hybrid (previous page). Sew a plain seam to join these edges, turn the whole inside-out and continue with the next tube. Final seam patterns are shown in Fig 4·9.

6 Cut two lengths of line approximately 320 cm (126 inches) and tie overhand loops at their centres. Tie the loose ends to the tips of the fins. Cut a third, much shorter length of line and thread it through the loops, tying it off with a suitable knot. Adjust the lines so that the inner ones are 148 cm (59¼ inches) and the outer ones 150 cm (60 inches) (Fig 4·10).

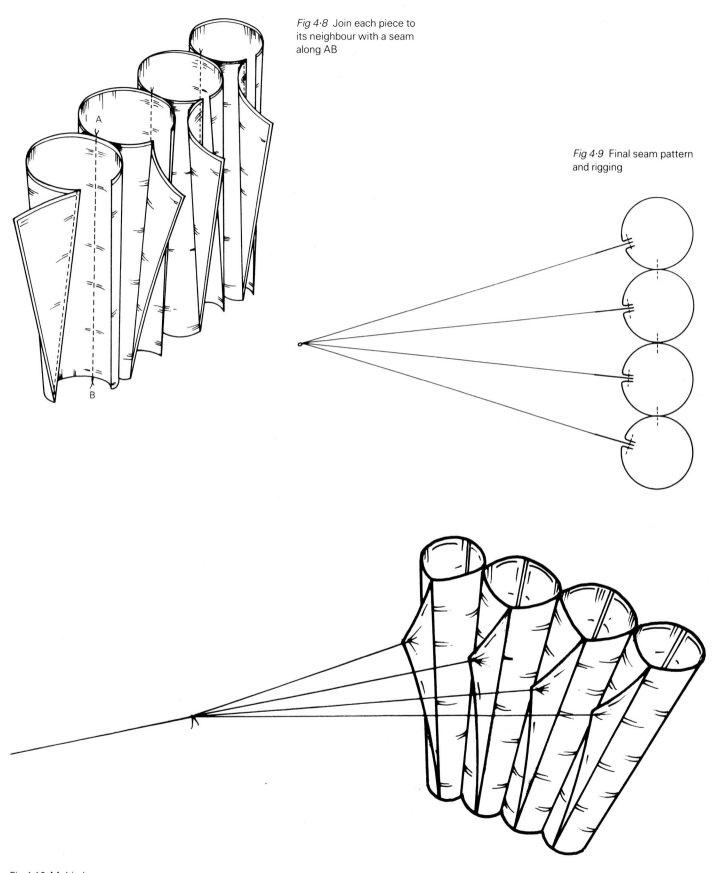

Fig 4·8 Join each piece to its neighbour with a seam along AB

Fig 4·9 Final seam pattern and rigging

Fig 4·10 Multitube complete

Parafoils

PARAFOIL 1: TWO-CELL

This is a simple parafoil which can be made in a few hours. The construction method used here follows that described in Chapter 3, to which you should also refer.

Materials

Fabric: 2 metres of 40–60 gm (2¼ yds of 1·25 oz) rip-stop nylon (balloon-quality fabric)
Rigging lines: 5 metres (5 yds) braided polyester
Flying line: 30 kg (70 lb) polyester

Construction

1 Mark and cut out the fabric pieces as shown: front, back, and three of each of the flares (Fig 5·1a–c). Using the measurements given in Table 1, make a template to mark and cut out five ribs (Fig 5·2).

2 Bind the edges of the flares and the forward edges of each of the ribs. Bind the forward edges of the front and back. Using the dimensions in Fig 5·3 (overleaf) draw chalk lines across the span of the kite (front) to assist the positioning of the flare tips.

Table 1: Aerofoil

Distance from leading edge	Height of upper surface
cm	cm
0·0	7·0
2·5	9·5
5·0	11·0
7·5	12·5
10·0	13·0
15·0	14·0
20·0	14·5
25·0	14·0
30·0	13·5
40·0	11·5
50·0	8·0
60·0	5·0
70·0	1·5
77·0	0·0

Table 2: Rigging

Flares

	2	1	2
A	71·5 cm	71 cm	71·5 cm
B	70·5 cm	70 cm	70·5 cm

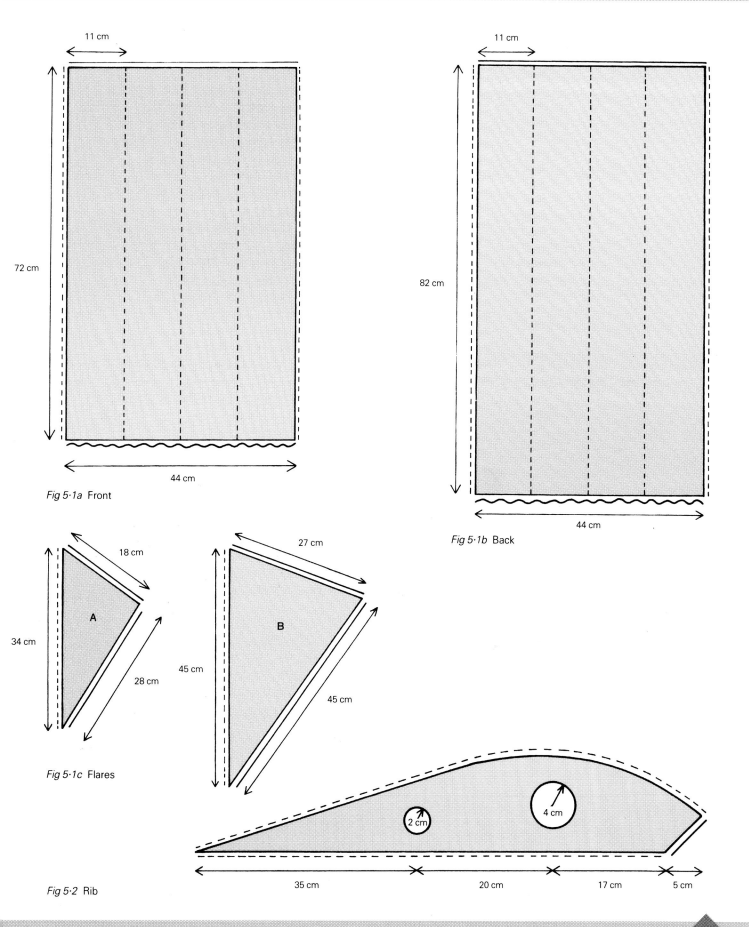

11 cm

72 cm

44 cm

Fig 5·1a Front

11 cm

82 cm

44 cm

Fig 5·1b Back

18 cm

A

34 cm

28 cm

Fig 5·1c Flares

27 cm

B

45 cm

45 cm

2 cm

4 cm

35 cm

20 cm

17 cm

5 cm

Fig 5·2 Rib

Fig 5·3 Flare positions

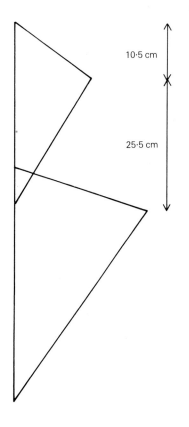

10·5 cm

25·5 cm

3 Sew the inner ribs to the front. Sew short tape loops to the tips of each of the flares before sewing the central ones in position.

4 Sew the outer flares in position, followed by the outer ribs.

5 Begin to sew the back. Starting from the next-to-outermost rib on one side, work to the other side.

6 As described on pages 28–9, roll the kite up from one side to leave two loose edges (those of the rib and the back). Bring these two loose edges together to enclose the roll and sew a plain seam.

7 Turn the tube inside out, and roll again to sew at the other side.

8 Close the bottom edge of the kite either with a double-fold hem, if you have allowed sufficient fabric, or bind it using a broad binding tape, again following the instructions given on page 29.

Rigging

9 Flat rig using the line dimensions given in Table 2 (page 36). The two-cell is usually able to fly without the need of a drogue, but if you find one necessary, tie it to tape loops sewn to the bottom corners of the kite (Fig 5·4). See also Chapter 9 on drogues.

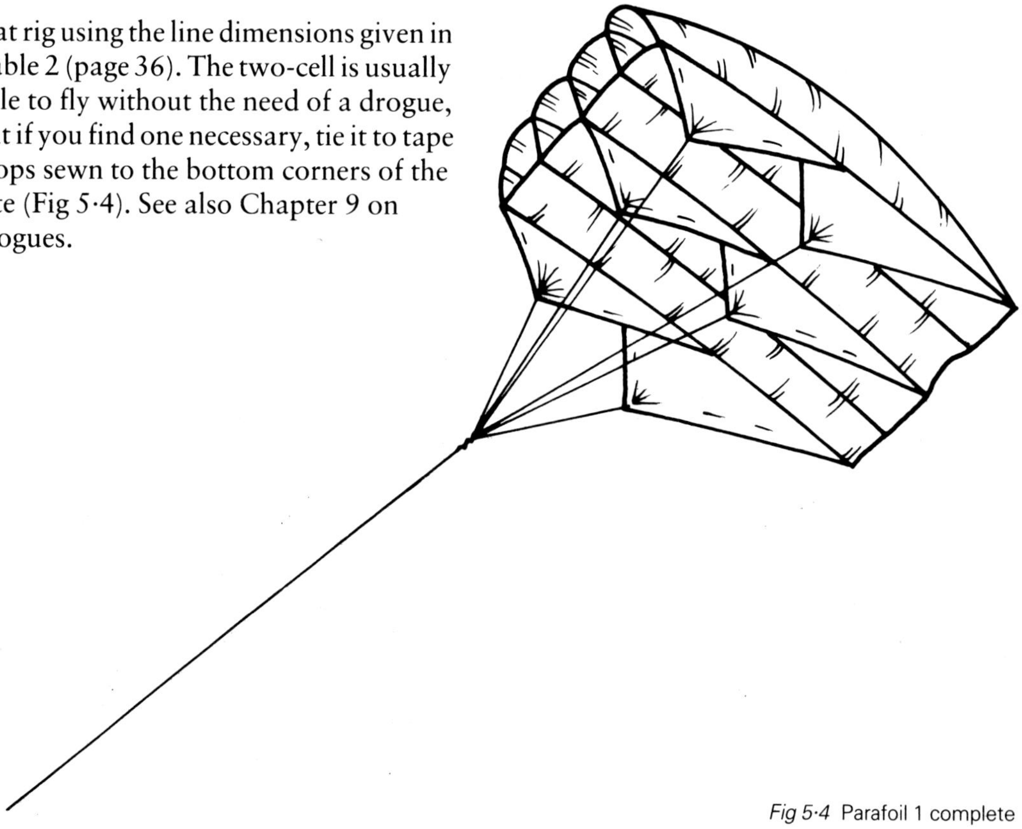

Fig 5·4 Parafoil 1 complete

PARAFOIL 2: THREE-CELL

This square, three-cell parafoil is very
similar to the previous design, but uses a
slightly different aerofoil section. For its
size the kite is a good lifter and fairly
reliable, but dislikes very strong gusts.
Parafoil 2 should be able to fly without a
drogue.

Materials

Fabric: 4 metres of 40–60 gm (4 yds of
  1.25 oz) rip-stop nylon (balloon fabric)
Rigging lines: 18 metres (20 yds) braided
  polyester
Flying line: 40 kg (90 lb) polyester

Table 1: Aerofoil

Distance from leading edge	Height of upper surface
cm	cm
0·0	9·0
2·5	11·0
5·0	12·5
7·5	14·0
10·0	15·5
15·0	17·0
20·0	17·0
30·0	15·0
40·0	12·5
50·0	9·5
60·0	7·0
70·0	4·0
80·0	1·5
85·0	0·0

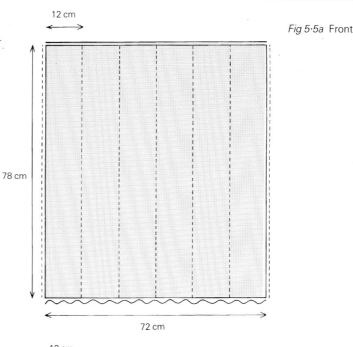

Fig 5·5a Front

12 cm

78 cm

72 cm

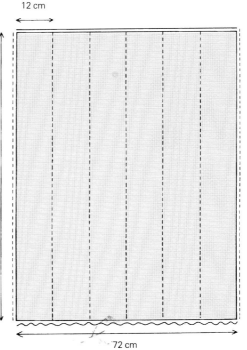

Fig 5·5b Back

12 cm

92 cm

72 cm

Table 2: Rigging

Flares

	2	1	1	2
A	135·5 cm	134 cm	134 cm	135·5 cm
B	129·5 cm	128 cm	128 cm	129·5 cm
C	133·5 cm	132 cm	132 cm	133·5 cm

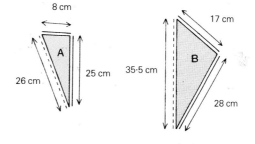

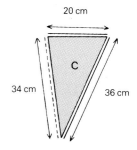

Fig 5·5c Flares

8 cm

A

26 cm   25 cm

17 cm

B

35·5 cm   28 cm

20 cm

C

34 cm   36 cm

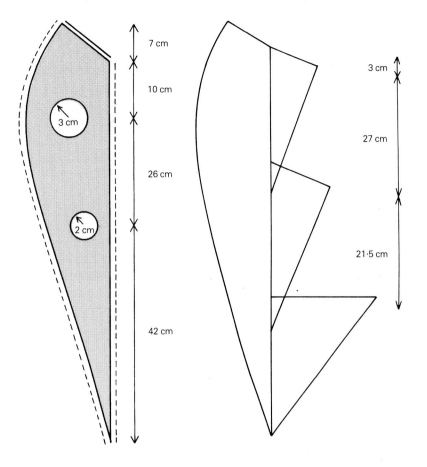

7 cm

10 cm

26 cm

42 cm

3 cm

2 cm

Fig 5·6 Rib

3 cm

27 cm

21·5 cm

Fig 5·7 Flare positions

Construction

1 The construction again follows the general method described in Chapter 3, to which you should refer.

2 Mark and cut out the fabric pieces as indicated: back, front, and five of each of three flares (Fig 5·5a–c). Using the details given in Table 1, make a template and mark and cut out nine ribs, of which seven should include inter-cell vents (Fig 5·6).

3 Bind the forward edges of the ribs, the back, front and two edges of each of the flares. Sew tape ties to the tips of the flares.

4 Sew the inner ribs to the front, then all the flares. Using the dimensions in Fig 5·7 make marks across the span to indicate the positions of the flare tips, and sew them to the front. Sew the outer ribs in position.

5 Join the back and the ribs as described in Chapter 3.

6 Close the trailing edge using a hem fold or binding tape (see page 29).

7 Flat rig with line dimensions as indicated in Table 2 (Fig 5·8).

Fig 5·8 Parafoil 2 complete

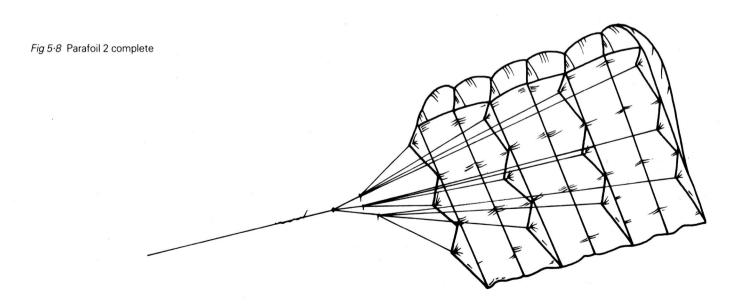

MAR (MEDIUM-ASPECT-RATIO) PARAFOIL

This kite was designed primarily to illustrate the concept of bifurcation in parafoil rigging. Bifurcation is the method of cascading the lines in order to reduce the total length required, which in turn reduces the line drag and the total weight of the system. Most modern parachutes feature cascaded lines, although they are less common on parafoils.

The MAR parafoil is unfortunately a kite which takes a lot of getting used to, as, near the ground without the support of a drogue, it is extremely unpredictable. In the sky it is, on the other hand, quite steady, flying at a high angle of elevation.

Materials

Fabric: 4·5 metres of 40–60 gm (5 yds of 1·25 oz) rip-stop nylon (balloon-quality)
Rigging lines: 45 metres (50 yds) braided polyester
Flying line: 150 kg (300 lb) polyester
Drogue

Construction

1 Mark and cut out the front, back and nine of each flare shape (Fig 5·9a–c). Using Table 1 (overleaf), make a template and mark and cut out seventeen ribs, fifteen of which should include inter-cell vents (Fig 5·10, overleaf).

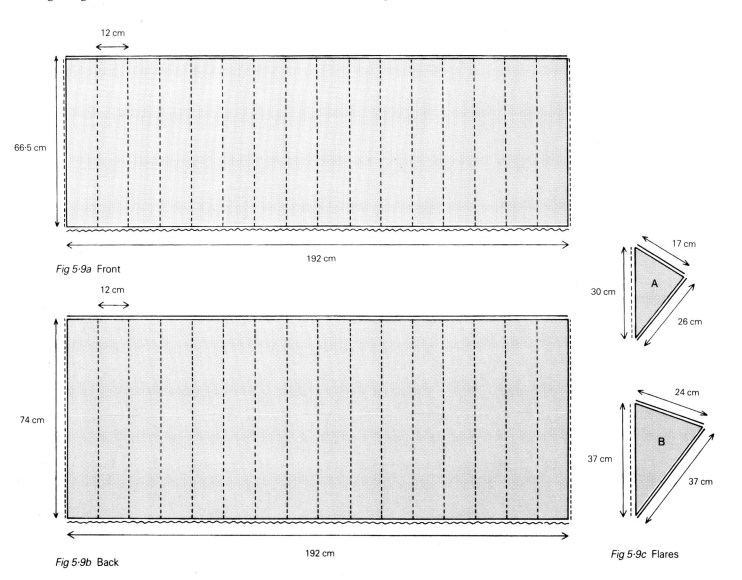

12 cm

66·5 cm

192 cm

Fig 5·9a Front

12 cm

74 cm

192 cm

Fig 5·9b Back

17 cm

30 cm   A   26 cm

24 cm

37 cm   B   37 cm

Fig 5·9c Flares

Fig 5·10 Rib

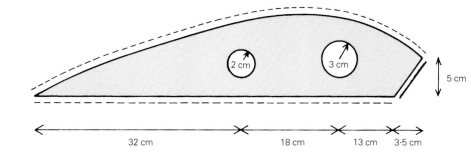

2 cm

3 cm

5 cm

32 cm   18 cm   13 cm   3·5 cm

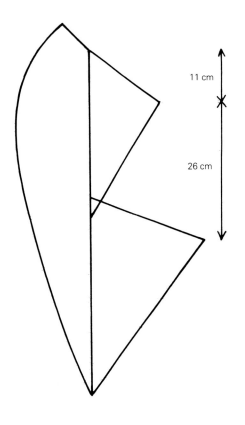

11 cm

26 cm

Fig 5·11 Flare positions

2 The construction then follows the general procedure described in Chapter 3.

3 Flare positions are indicated in Fig 5·11.

Table 1: Aerofoil

Distance from leading edge	Height of upper surface
cm	cm
0·0	6·0
2·5	9·0
5·0	11·0
7·5	12·0
10·0	12·5
15·0	12·5
20·0	12·0
30·0	11·0
40·0	8·0
50·0	5·0
60·0	2·0
70·0	0·0

Rigging

4 Cut nine lengths of line 175 cm (69 inches) long and tie overhand loops at their centres. Tie the loose ends to each set of flares and adjust them so that the upper legs are 80 cm (31½ inches) long and the lower legs 81 cm (32 inches). To adjust them to the required lengths you may find it helpful to thread a short length of stick through the loops and compare the legs with each of their neighbours, adjusting as necessary (Fig 5·12). Although the kite will tolerate bridle dimensions slightly different from those indicated, it will not tolerate differences across the span.

5 Cut a further nine lengths of line and tie overhand loops at one end of each. Tie the other end through the loops on the primary lines and adjust the length of each to 380 cm (150 inches). Tie a third line through the loops to bring them together to provide a suitable towing point (Fig 5·13, overleaf).

6 As it has such a high-aspect ratio, this kite really does need a drogue to maintain stability. Sew short tape loops to points on the trailing edge, 24 cm (9½ inches) each side of the centre, from which to tie the drogue lines (Figs 5·14 and 5·15, overleaf).

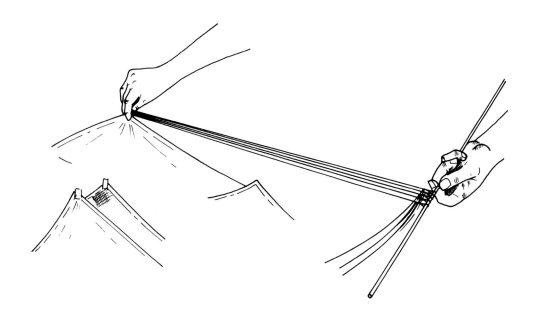

Fig 5·12 Thread a short stick through the loops to check line lengths

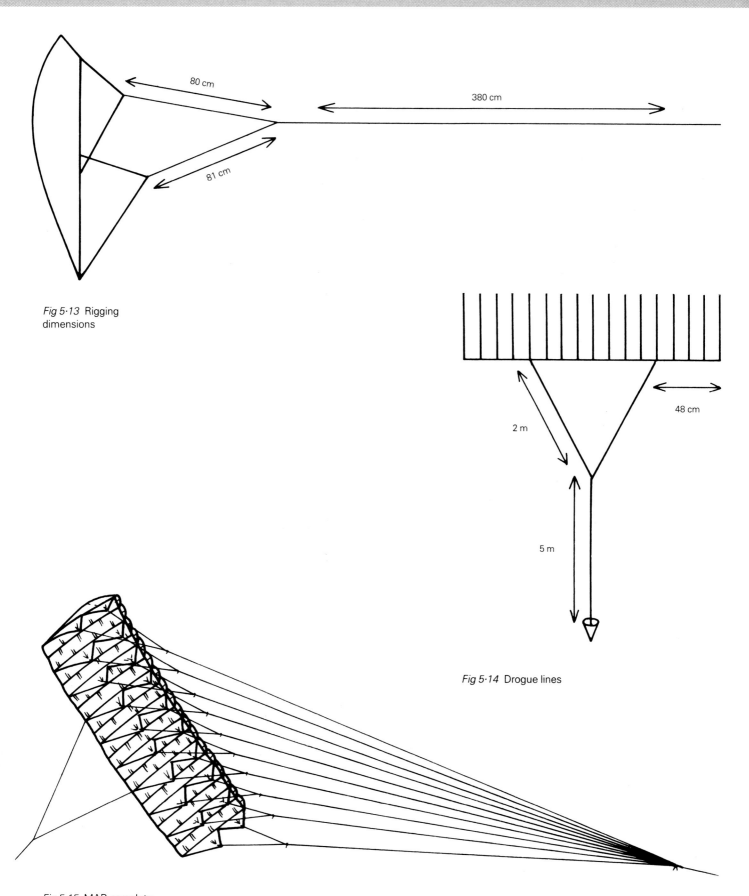

Fig 5·13 Rigging
dimensions

Fig 5·14 Drogue lines

Fig 5·15 MAR complete

PARASLED Z

In the years following the introduction of the parafoil, Domina Jalbert continued his development of this design with a parachute which he described as the Aerial Sled. This comprised a basic parafoil form, but with a rounded nose and the forward edge covered by a mesh. There were also valves on the lower surface which opened and closed to allow air to enter and leave the body of the kite. The object of such modifications was to maintain the pressure in the body of the kite at a constant level, thereby improving its shape, performance and stability.

Unfortunately the Aerial Sled never received the same attention as the parafoil, but the concept of closing the forward edge and introducing air via vents, or valves on the lower surface, has been used on many other designs, notably on Dave Green's Stratoscoops and, more recently, on kites by Peter Lynn. Through general misunderstanding and misuse the term 'parasled' has, however, come to mean any parafoil having a closed leading edge.

In terms of aerodynamics, the great difference between parasleds and parafoils is in the shape of the nose. To create a suitable air inlet the nose on the parafoil is sharp or more precisely truncated, which creates a large amount of drag. But by providing a smaller air inlet, through mesh, the nose of the parasled can be rounded, significantly reducing the amount of drag and improving performance.

As the back and front are made from a single piece of fabric, the construction of the parasled is more complex than the standard parafoil.

Materials

Fabric: 5 metres of 40–60 gm (5 yds of 1·25 oz) rip-stop nylon (balloon-quality)
1 metre x 15 cm (1 yd x 6 inches) light nylon mesh
Rigging lines: 27 metres (30 yds) braided polyester
Flying line: 40 kg (90 lb) polyester

Table 1: Aerofoil

Distance from leading edge	Lower surface	Upper surface
cm	cm	cm
0·0	7·5	7·5
2·5	2·5	12·0
5·0	1·0	14·5
7·5	0·0	16·5
10·0	0·0	17·5
15·0	0·0	19·0
20·0	0·0	19·5
25·0	0·0	20·0
30·0	0·0	19·0
40·0	0·0	17·5
50·0	0·0	15·5
60·0	0·0	13·0
70·0	0·0	10·0
80·0	0·0	7·0
90·0	0·0	4·0
100·0	0·0	0·0

Table 2: Rigging

Flares

	3	2	1	2	3
A	170 cm	165 cm	163 cm	165 cm	170 cm
B	165 cm	159 cm	157 cm	159 cm	165 cm
C	162 cm	157 cm	155 cm	157 cm	162 cm

Construction

1 The body panel should be made as a single piece (Fig 5·16a, overleaf). Mark and cut out five of each of the flares (Fig 5·16b) and nine ribs, only seven of which should have inter-cell vents (Fig 5·17). Bind the forward edges of the flares and sew small tape loops to their tips, as with previous designs.

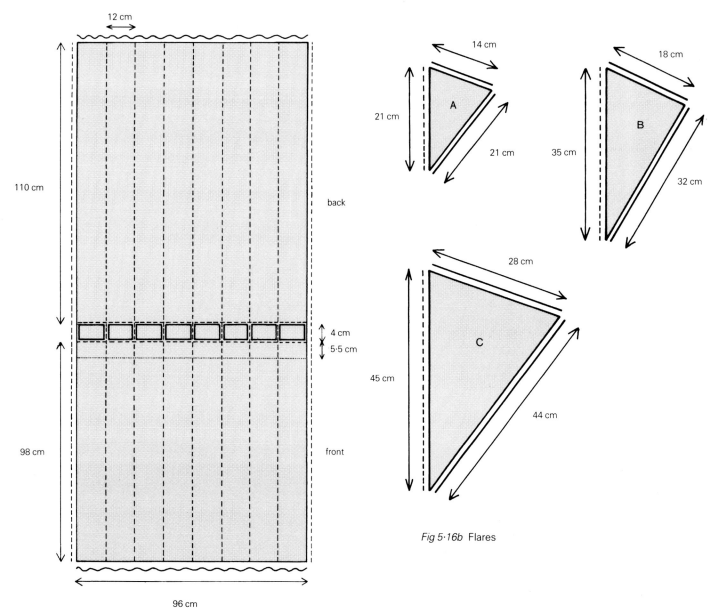

12 cm

110 cm

back

4 cm
5·5 cm

98 cm

front

96 cm

Fig 5·16a Single body
piece

14 cm

21 cm

A

21 cm

18 cm

35 cm

B

32 cm

28 cm

45 cm

C

44 cm

Fig 5·16b Flares

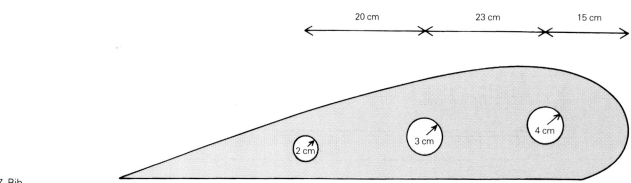

20 cm

23 cm

15 cm

2 cm

3 cm

4 cm

Fig 5·17 Rib

2 The mesh is applied in a similar manner to cut-away appliqué (see page 23). Mark the position and shape of the forward vents on the right side of the body panel. Cut a large single piece of nylon mesh, slightly wider than the proposed vents and as long as the span of the kite, then tape or glue it to the wrong side of the fabric. Sew along the lines previously drawn and, when complete, cut away the part of the sail to allow the mesh to show through (Fig 5·18).

3 It is important that the forward opening – the mesh – sits at the correct position in relation to the nose curvature. Too far back or too far forward and either the nose will collapse or the kite will not inflate properly. To achieve this, using the rib template, make a mark on the lower edge of each rib, 10 cm (4 inches) from the forward (nose) end. Transfer this mark to each of the ribs.

4 Mark what will be the corresponding position on the body panel 5·5 cm (2¼ inches) from the marked mesh opening (Fig 5·16a).

5 To add the ribs, match up the marked points on the rib with the corresponding point on the body panel and sew the rib from this point towards the trailing edge of the kite. Sew all but the outer ribs (**Fig 5·19**).

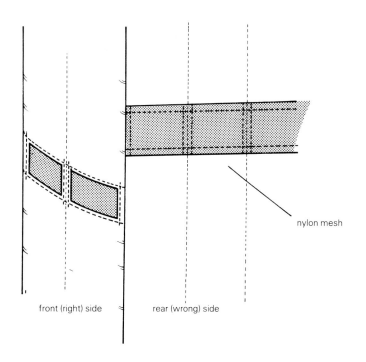

front (right) side   rear (wrong) side

nylon mesh

Fig 5·18 Sew a nylon mesh to create the forward vent

Fig 5·19 Match the marked points on the rib to the corresponding points on the body piece

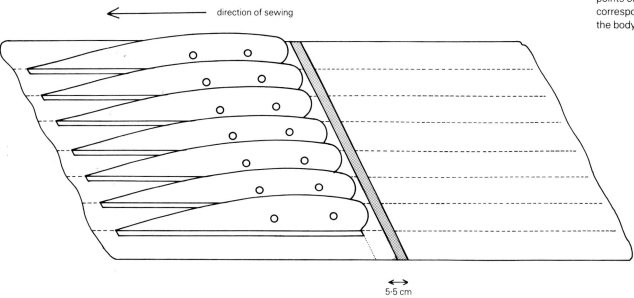

direction of sewing

5·5 cm

Fig 5·20 Flare positions

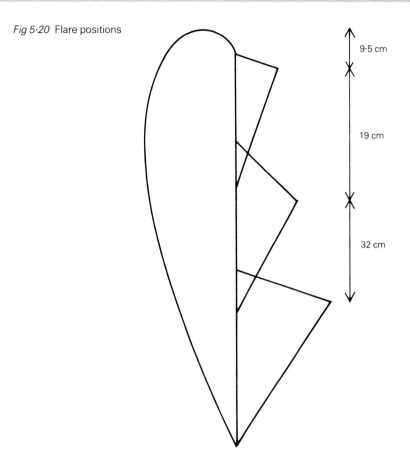

9·5 cm

19 cm

32 cm

6 Sew the flares to the front using a similar procedure to previous designs. Flare positions are shown in Fig 5·20.

7 From one side, complete the stitching of the ribs round the nose, down the back to the trailing edge. Sewing the nose is the most difficult part, and accuracy rather than haste is most important here.

8 The outer ribs are sewn in a similar fashion to previous designs. From one side roll the kite up and fold the two edges – rib and back – to enclose the rest of the kite. Sew a plain seam. Turn the whole inside-out and repeat from the other side.

9 Close the trailing edge with a double-fold hem or with binding tape, as preferred (see page 29).

10 Flat rig with the line dimensions given in Table 2 (page 45).

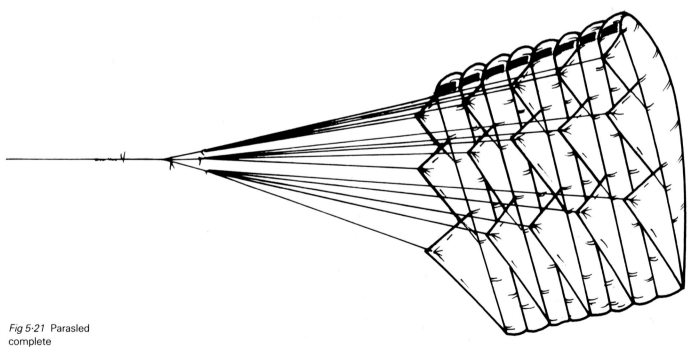

Fig 5·21 Parasled complete

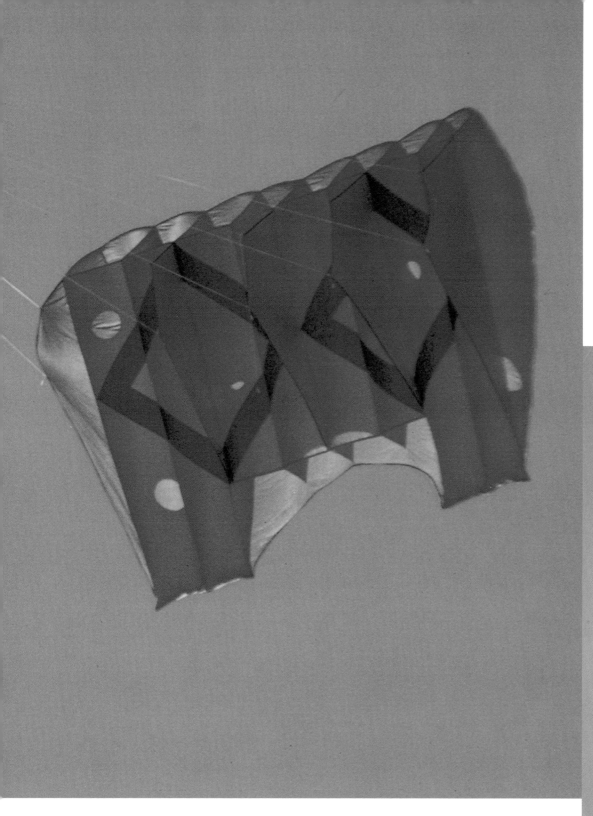

Flowform

Soldier (Ann Megrath)

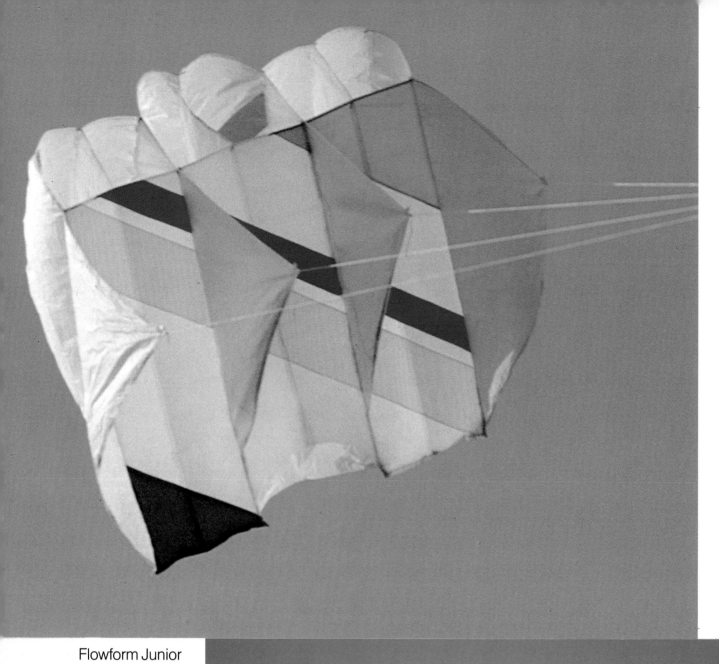

Flowform Junior

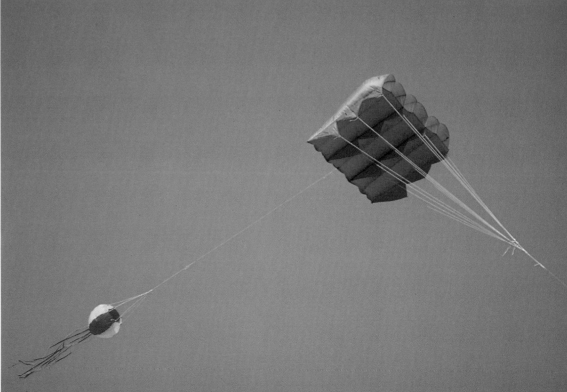

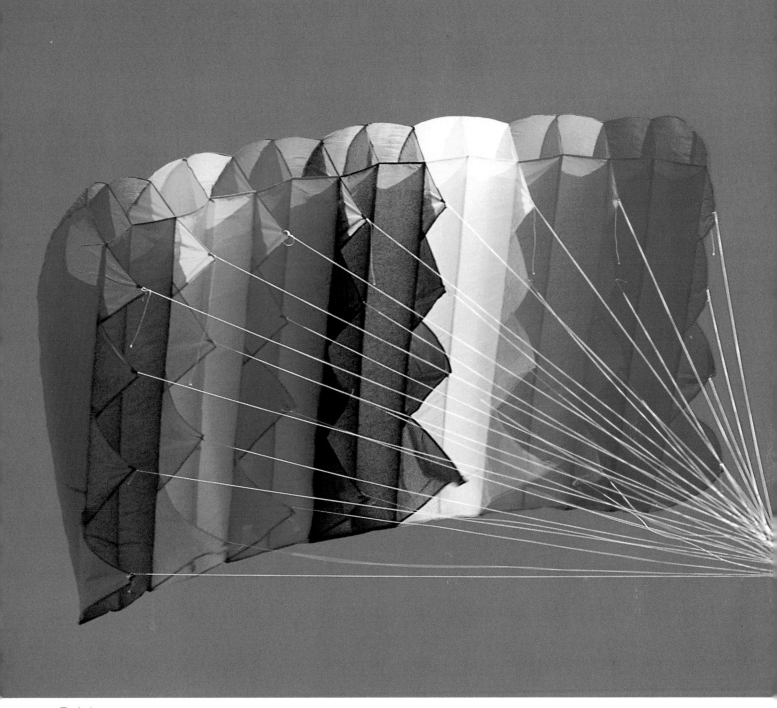

Rainbow

Three-cell parafoil with pumpkin drogue

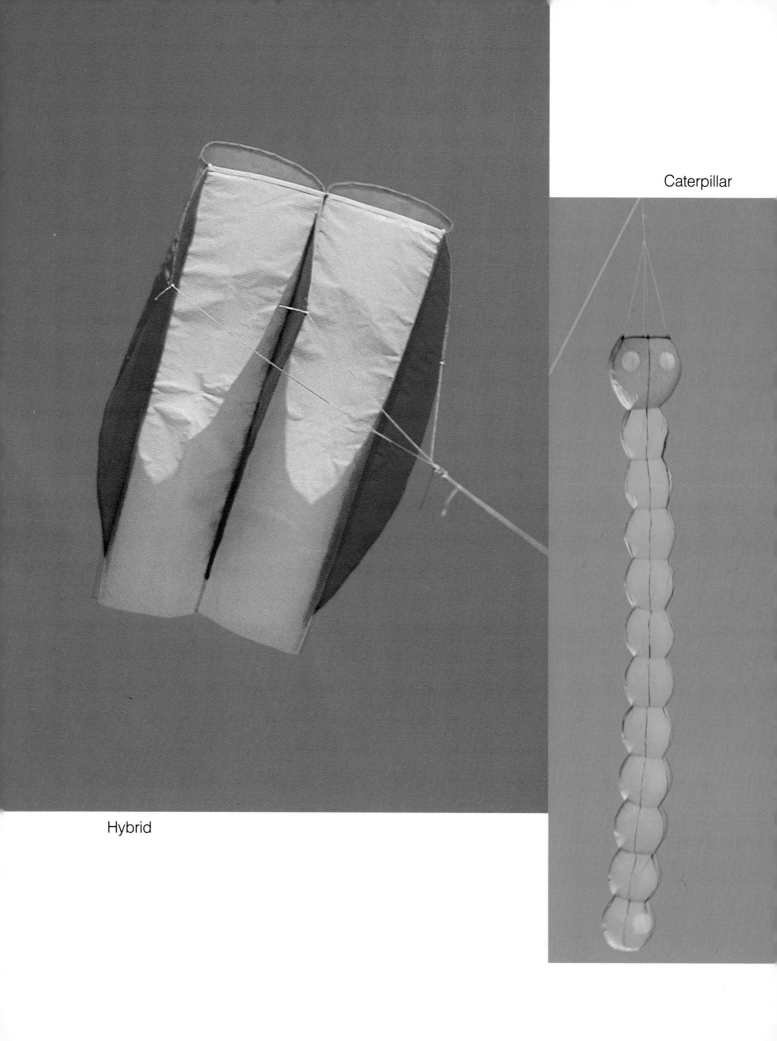

Caterpillar

Hybrid

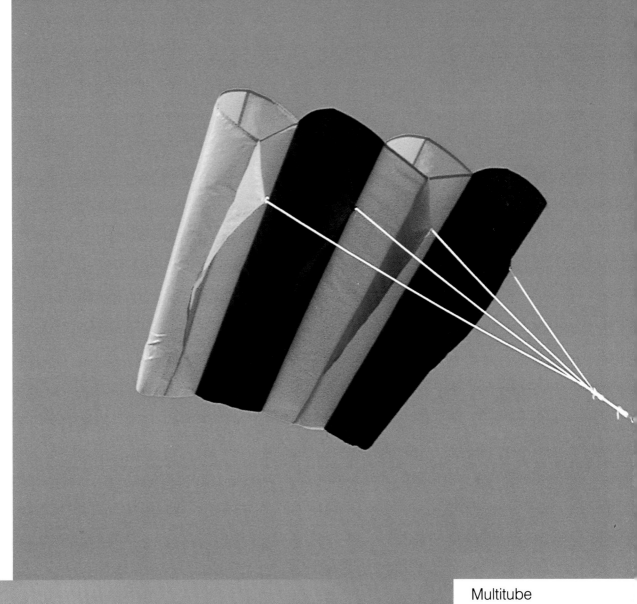

Frog

Multitube

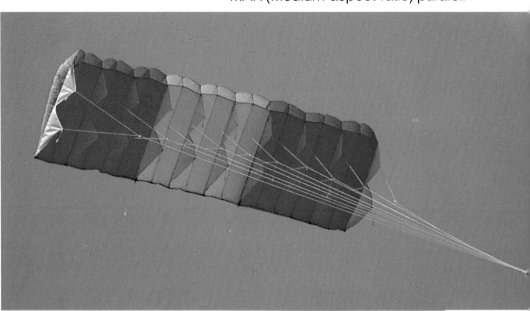

MAR (Medium-aspect-ratio) parafoil

Flowform Junior

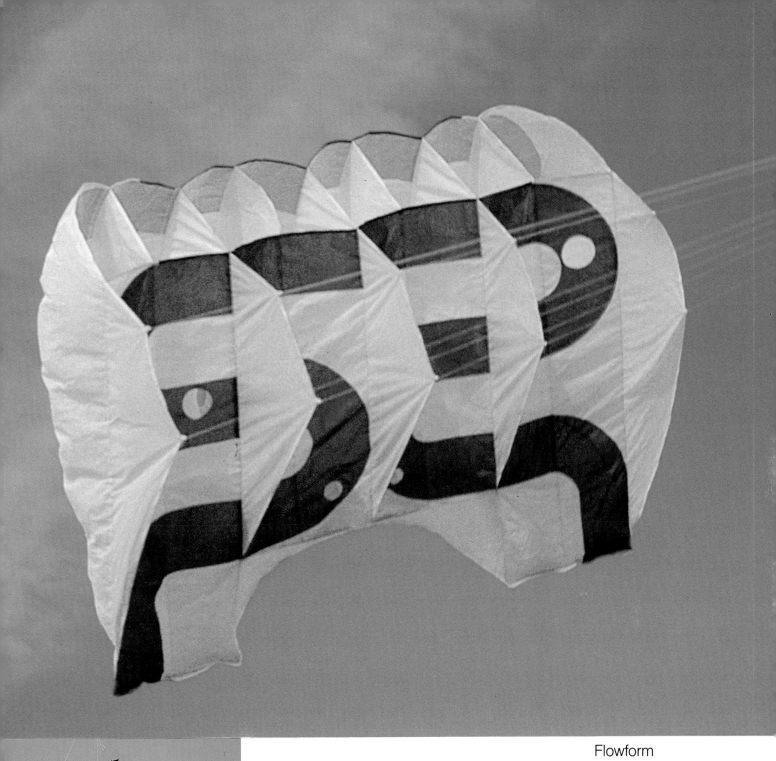

Flowform

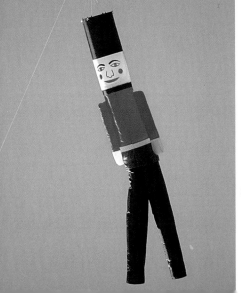

Soldier

Whale

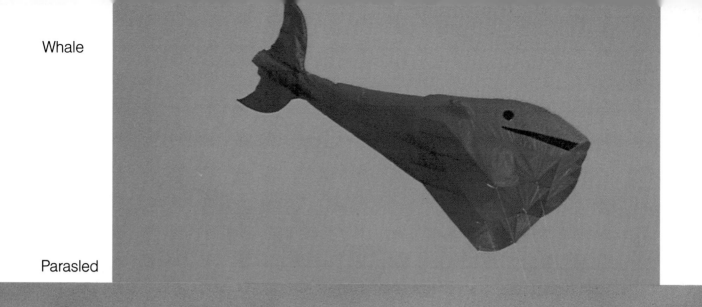

Parasled

CROWN-RIGGED RAINBOW

The Rainbow differs from most other designs featured, not only in the construction technique but more particularly in the method of rigging.

In previous designs, the lines attached to the outer flares are longer than those nearer the centres, enabling the kite to form a flat wing. The Rainbow, however, is crown-rigged: that is, lines attached at the same chord position – the A lines, for example – are all the same length, and rather than a flat wing the kite forms an anhedralled arc, the outer edges curving forwards towards the flier.

Rigging the kite now becomes much simpler, but to achieve this arc without the whole canopy collapsing, the back must be made wider than the front and the edges of each panel contoured to accommodate the shape of the aerofoil. There are several ways of achieving the contour, but the easiest is to construct the back as seven separate pieces. For my prototype I chose the colours of the rainbow – violet, pale blue, blue, green, yellow, orange and red.

The Rainbow is a large, powerful and potentially dangerous kite and it should only be flown with extreme care. Except in very light winds it should always be anchored, never hand-held, and launching should be supervised by at least two people.

Materials

Fabric: 12 metres of 40–60 gm (14 yds of 1·25 oz) rip-stop nylon (balloon-quality)
Rigging lines: 85 metres of 50 kg (90 yds of 100 lb) Dacron
Flying line: 300 kg (700 lb) polyester or Dacron

Table 1: Aerofoil

Distance from leading edge	Height of upper surface
cm	cm
0·0	16·0
5·0	20·5
10·0	23·0
15·0	25·0
20·0	27·0
30·0	28·5
40·0	29·0
50·0	28·0
60·0	27·0
70·0	25·0
80·0	23·0
100·0	17·5
120·0	12·0
140·0	5·0
150·0	0·0

Table 2: Rigging

Flares

A	250 cm
B	250 cm
C	255 cm
D	254 cm

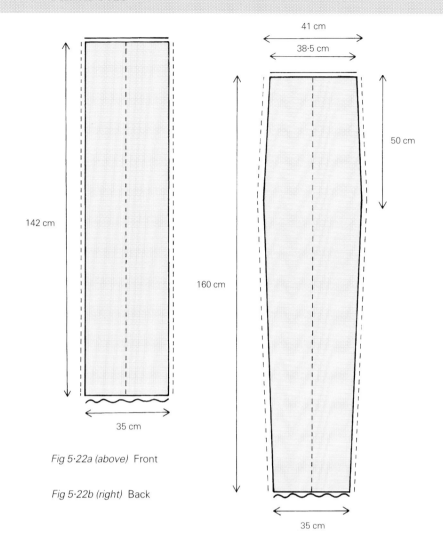

142 cm

35 cm

Fig 5·22a (above) Front

Fig 5·22b (right) Back

41 cm

38·5 cm

50 cm

160 cm

35 cm

Construction

1 Mark and cut out seven of each of the panels which make up the back and front (Fig 5·22a and b). Bind or hem the forward edges.

2 Use the measurements given in Table 1 to make the template, and mark and cut out fifteen ribs. Cut inter-cellular vents in all but two of these, and, as with previous designs, bind or hem the forward edges as preferred (Fig 5·23).

3 Cut out the flares, eight from each pattern. Bind or hem the edges and sew short tape loops to their tips (Fig 5·24).

4 Join the seven back pieces along the curved edges using a plain seam.

5 The front is made up cell by cell. Using the dimensions given in Fig 5·25, mark lines on each of the front panels to indicate the position of the flare tips, and join each to its neighbour sandwiching the flares in between (Fig 5·26).

6 Sew all the ribs to the front and continue to add the back to complete the kite. A suggested seam pattern is indicated in Fig 5·27.

7 Close the trailing edge either with a double-fold hem or binding tape (see page 29).

8 Add rigging lines using the dimensions given in Table 2 (previous page).

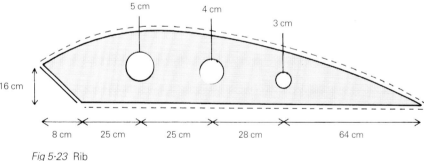

5 cm

4 cm

3 cm

16 cm

8 cm   25 cm   25 cm   28 cm   64 cm

Fig 5·23 Rib

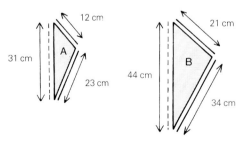

12 cm

A

31 cm

23 cm

21 cm

B

44 cm

34 cm

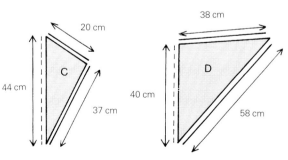

20 cm

C

44 cm

37 cm

38 cm

D

40 cm

58 cm

Fig 5·24 Flares

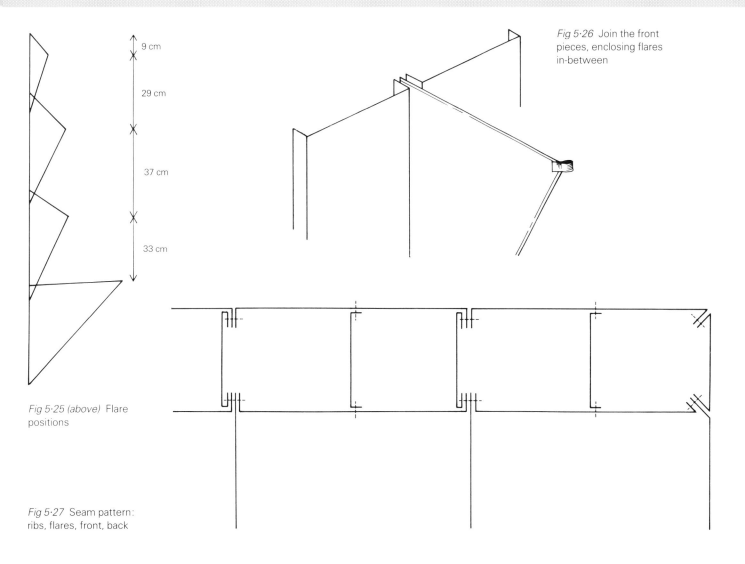

9 cm

29 cm

37 cm

33 cm

Fig 5·26 Join the front pieces, enclosing flares in-between

Fig 5·25 (above) Flare positions

Fig 5·27 Seam pattern: ribs, flares, front, back

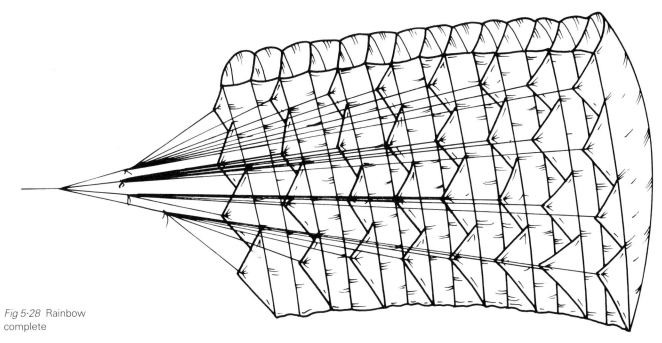

Fig 5·28 Rainbow complete

Flowforms

The Flowform is a particular type of parafoil developed in the late 1960s by Canadian parachutist Steven Sutton. It differs from the Jalbert design in several important features.

Conventional parafoils rely for many of their characteristics on the maintenance of an equal pressure in each of the cells. With the kite inclined at the correct angle, air enters the forward, open edge of the canopy which then starts to inflate. As inflation increases, the air pressure inside soon rises above that of the oncoming wind, and any further air pushing on the open edge of the kite is spilled over the upper and lower surfaces, thereby providing the necessary lifting forces. In this state the kite is aerodynamically similar to the wing of an aircraft.

If the wind momentarily changes direction, as it might do in gusty conditions, the local angle of attack will change, perhaps increasing beyond stall, and may also vary across the span. As a result the kite will become unstable and start to roll. At the same time the pressure in the cells may also change, causing slight differences in the aerofoil shape from cell to cell, which may aggravate the rolling motion further.

The Flowform is designed so that this instability can be overcome. The forward opening is much larger than on the standard parafoil, and the trailing edge of the central cells is also open. To assist air flow between cells, large vents are cut into the ribs, and additional vents are cut in upper and lower surfaces in a V-shape pattern. These vents can act as both air-entry and -exit points depending on the local surface pressure, and provide the main clue to how the Flowform works.

Firstly, air flow through the vents on the upper surface delays stall and the consequent rapid fall-off in lift experienced with standard parafoils. Local increases in the angle of attack will consequently not have the same effect. Additionally, any changes in internal or external pressure due to changes in the wind speed or angle of attack are immediately compensated by air flow both through the inter-cell vents and those on the outer surfaces. The venting system is able to 'read' both the internal and external pressure, and allows air to flow in the required direction. The Flowform is consequently more able to cope with variable wind conditions and remain in stable flight.

FLOWFORM JUNIOR

Although using the Flowform principle, this design dispenses with the pressure-flow vents on the upper and lower surfaces, and instead makes use of a very large central opening. Despite its small size it does have a strong pull, and will remain very steady, at a high angle of elevation, in all but the most gusty conditions.

Materials

Fabric: 5 metres of 40–60 gm (5 yds of 1·25 oz) rip-stop nylon (balloon-quality)
Rigging: 12 metres (14 yds) braided polyester
Flying line: 50 kg (100 lb) polyester

Construction

1 Mark and cut out the fabric pieces: back, two panels (Fig 6·1a); back centre, one panel (Fig 6·1b); front, two panels

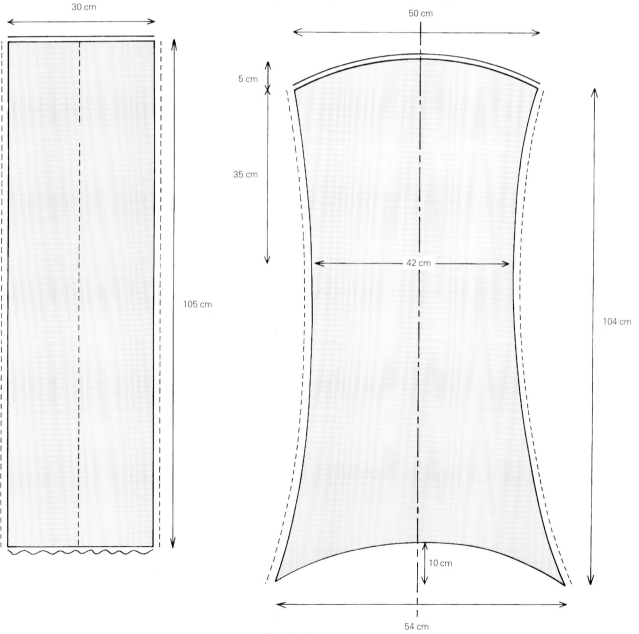

Fig 6·1a Back   Fig 6·1b Back centre

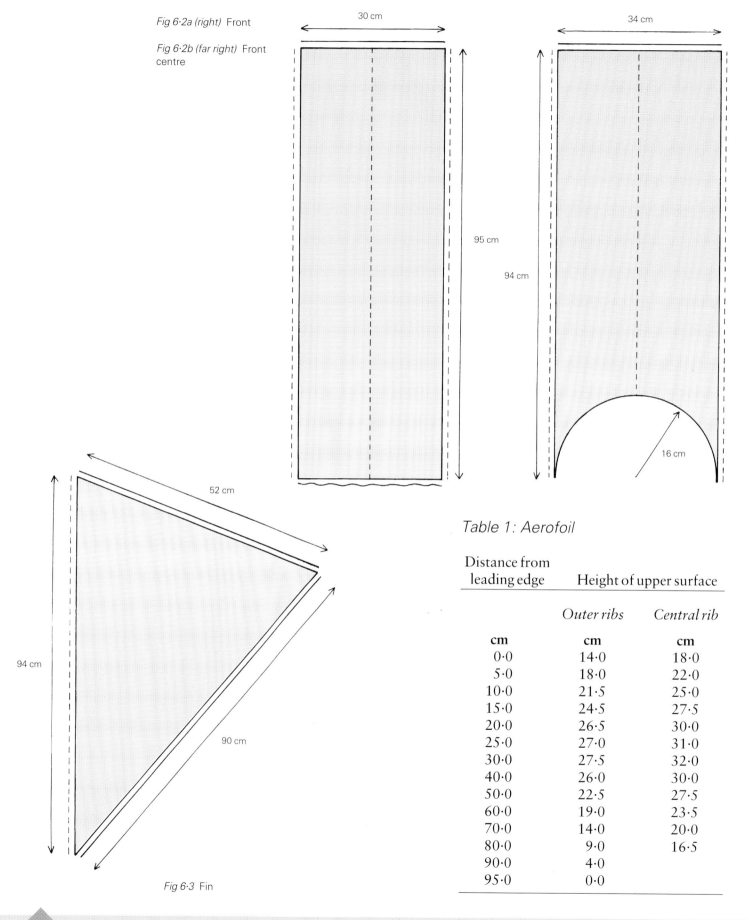

Fig 6·2a (right) Front

Fig 6·2b (far right) Front centre

30 cm

34 cm

95 cm

94 cm

16 cm

52 cm

94 cm

90 cm

Fig 6·3 Fin

Table 1: Aerofoil

Distance from leading edge	Height of upper surface	
	Outer ribs	Central rib
cm	cm	cm
0·0	14·0	18·0
5·0	18·0	22·0
10·0	21·5	25·0
15·0	24·5	27·5
20·0	26·5	30·0
25·0	27·0	31·0
30·0	27·5	32·0
40·0	26·0	30·0
50·0	22·5	27·5
60·0	19·0	23·5
70·0	14·0	20·0
80·0	9·0	16·5
90·0	4·0	
95·0	0·0	

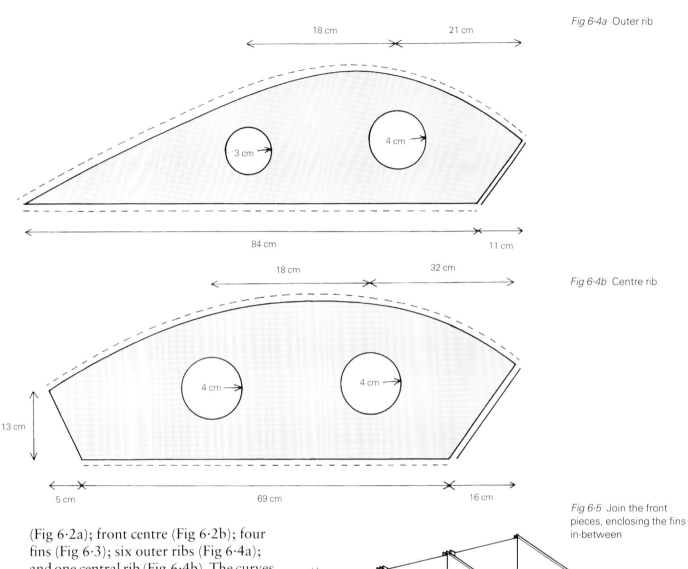

Fig 6·4a Outer rib

18 cm   21 cm

3 cm   4 cm

84 cm   11 cm

Fig 6·4b Centre rib

18 cm   32 cm

4 cm   4 cm

13 cm

5 cm   69 cm   16 cm

Fig 6·5 Join the front pieces, enclosing the fins in-between

(Fig 6·2a); front centre (Fig 6·2b); four fins (Fig 6·3); six outer ribs (Fig 6·4a); and one central rib (Fig 6·4b). The curves on the trailing edges of both front and back central panels should preferably be hot cut to prevent fraying (see pages 16–17).

2 Bind the forward edges of the front and back sections, two outer edges of the fins and forward edges of the seven ribs. Sew a short tape loop to each of the fin tips.

3 Join the front left and right panels to the centre, enclosing the central flares in between. Do not trim the excess fabric on the seam edge yet. Sew the outer fins in position (Fig 6·5).

4 Join the left and right back panels to the back centre. Use a plain seam, and, again, do not trim excess fabric along the seam edge.

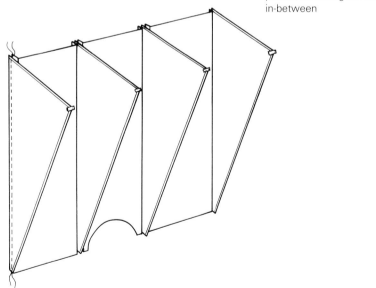

Fig 6·6 Seam pattern: ribs and fins

centre rib

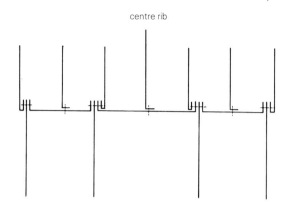

Fig 6·7 Seam pattern: ribs and back

centre rib

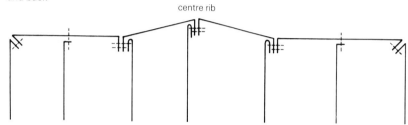

5 Sew the ribs, in turn, to the front. To create a neat edge the seam pattern shown in Fig 6·6 should be used.

6 Sew the ribs to the back section, starting from the centre and working outwards alternately on both sides (Fig 6·7). Sew the outer ribs to the back using the procedure described in Chapter 3. Trim off the excess fabric at the seam edges.

7 Close the bottom edge of each side using a wide binding tape.

8 Cut two lengths of line approximately 420 cm (170 inches) long, bring them together at their centres and tie an overhand loop. Tie the loose ends to the fin tips and adjust the length so that the outer legs are 205 cm (80 inches) long, and the inner legs 200 cm (78 inches) long (Fig 6·8).

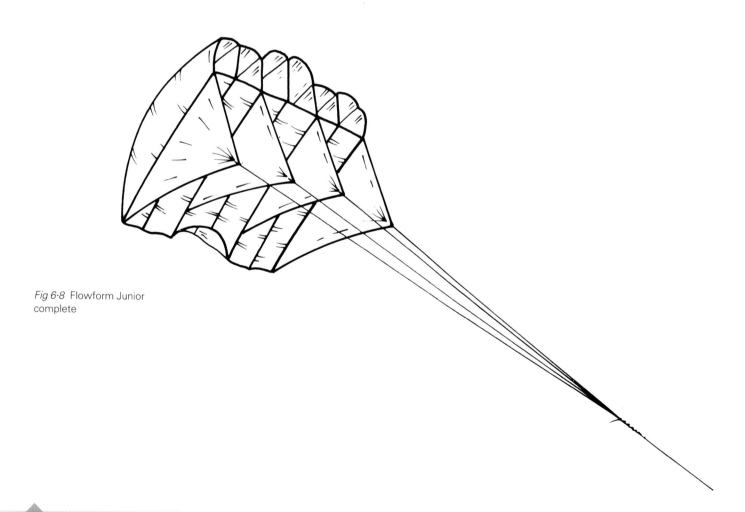

Fig 6·8 Flowform Junior complete

FLOWFORM

If I have a favourite kite, this has to be it. It is a kite which will fly in almost any wind, has excellent characteristics with a good lift, and is normally as steady as a rock. Useful for camera-lifting, as a windsock anchor or for parachuting fauna.

Materials

Fabric: 8 metres of 40–60 gm (9 yds of 1.25 oz) rip-stop nylon (balloon-quality)
Rigging lines: 40 metres (45 yds) braided polyester/Dacron
Flying line: 150 kg (300 lb) polyester

Table 1: Aerofoil

Distance from leading edge	Height of upper surface
cm	cm
0·0	22·5
5·0	26·0
10·0	29·5
15·0	32·0
20·0	34·0
30·0	36·5
40·0	37·0
50·0	35·0
60·0	32·0
80·0	23·0
100·0	12·5
120·0	2·0
125·0	0·0

Table 2: Rigging

Flares

	3	2	1	2	3
A	410 cm	402 cm	400 cm	402 cm	410 cm
B	410 cm	402 cm	400 cm	402 cm	410 cm

Construction

1 To achieve more efficient use of fabric, both the back and front should be made up from three separate pieces. Mark and cut out the front left and right (Fig 6·9a) and front centre (Fig 6·9b); the back left and right (Fig 6·10a, overleaf) and one back centre (Fig 6·10b). Bind or hem the edges as indicated.

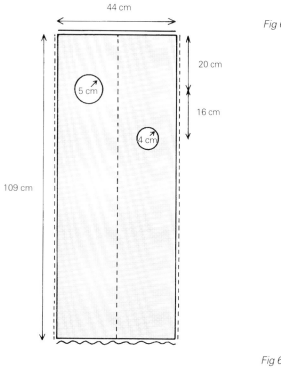

Fig 6·9a Front

Fig 6·9b Front centre

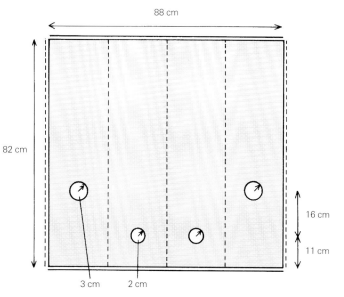

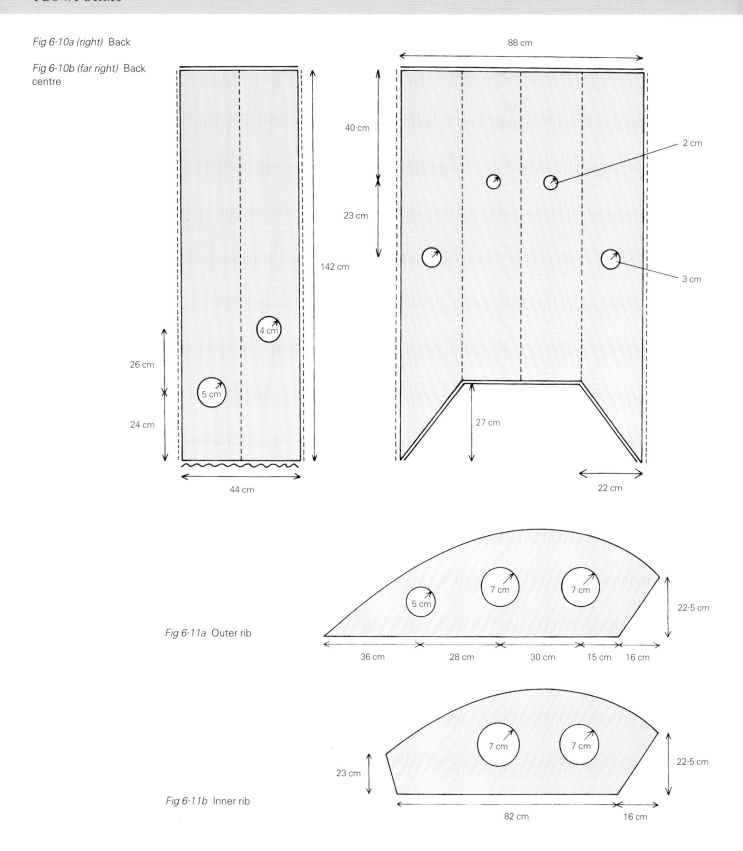

Fig 6·10a (right) Back

Fig 6·10b (far right) Back centre

88 cm

40 cm

2 cm

23 cm

3 cm

142 cm

4 cm

26 cm

5 cm

24 cm

27 cm

44 cm

22 cm

Fig 6·11a Outer rib

5 cm

7 cm

7 cm

22·5 cm

36 cm   28 cm   30 cm   15 cm   16 cm

7 cm

7 cm

22·5 cm

23 cm

Fig 6·11b Inner rib

82 cm   16 cm

2 Mark and cut out the vent holes; hot cutting is recommended.

3 Using the information in Table 1 mark and cut out six outer ribs (Fig 6·11a) and three inner ribs (Fig 6·11b). Make two outer flares (Fig 6·12a) and three inner flares (Fig 6·12b).

4 Bind or hem the edges as indicated. The procedure is then very similar to the Flowform Junior (pages 53–6).

5 Join the three front panels together, enclosing the flares between them. Add the central and outer flares.

6 Sew the ribs in position using the seam pattern suggested in Fig 6·13.

7 Sew the ribs to the back, working from the centre outwards. Ensure that the seam joining rib number three sits neatly on the inside (Fig 6·14, overleaf).

8 Close off the trailing edge with a broad binding tape (see page 29).

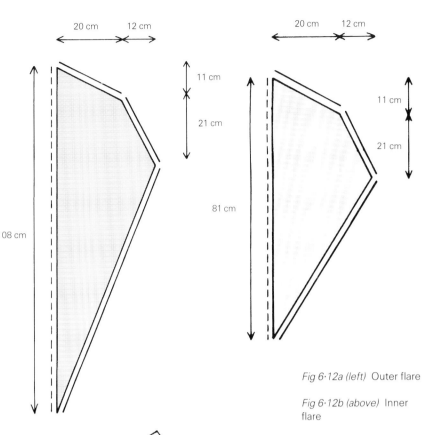

Fig 6·12a (left) Outer flare

Fig 6·12b (above) Inner flare

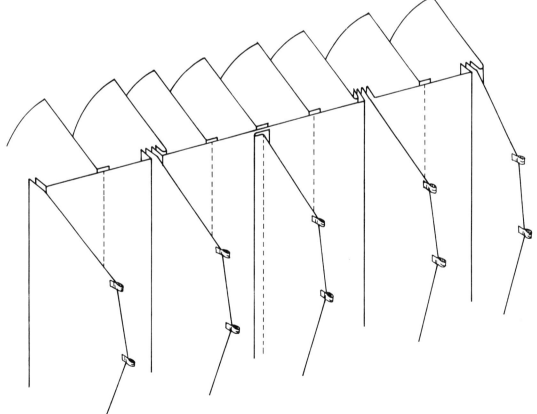

Fig 6·13 Seam pattern: front

9 The Flowform is flat-rigged with line dimensions as in Table 2 (page 57).

Fig 6·14 Seam pattern: front, ribs, flares and back

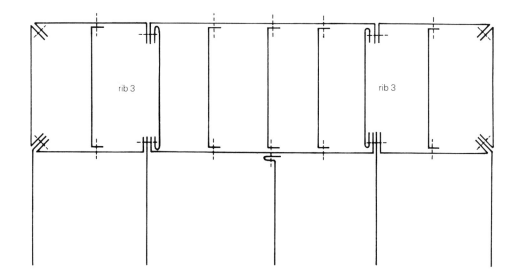

rib 3   rib 3

Fig 6·15 Flowform complete

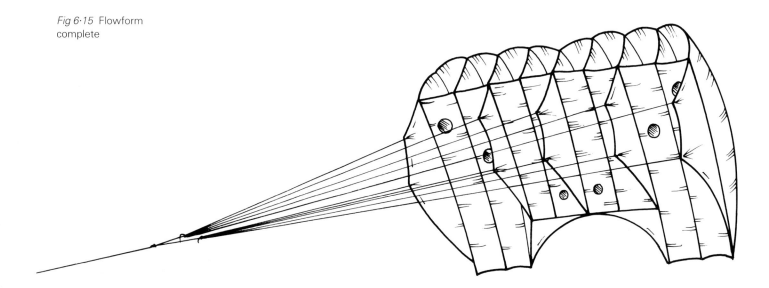

Fig 6·16 (right) Flowform kite with traveller for automatic release of parachuting teddies

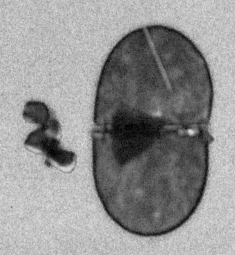
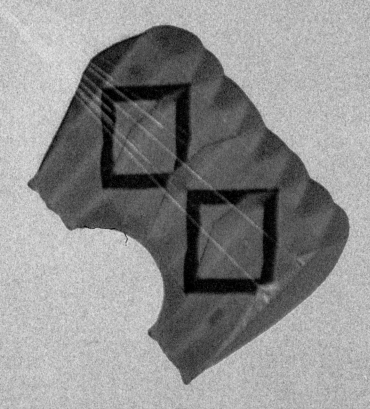

Inflatable Kites

Over the past five years, many designers have been giving their attention to a new category of kites described as inflatables. These kites are similar to the parafoil in that there are obvious upper and lower surfaces, shaped ribs and a forward air intake, but at the same time the variety of planforms, aerofoil sections and stabilizing devices is so different as to make them a separate group or species.

In most cases, the planforms take on the shape of some natural creature or object. Martin Lester's 'Legs', Peter Lynn's 'Octopus' or Peter Rielet's 'Superfly' are fairly representative examples of this new trend in kite design, mimicking the actions of these creatures running, swimming or flying.

The two kites featured here take up similar ideas. The whale, with its blunt nose and long, tapering body, and a tail which flicks to imitate breaching; and the frog, whose legs move in the wind as though it were leaping from stone to stone.

WHALE

Already regarded as a kite 'classic', the whale was designed for an environment-awareness festival taking place near my home. The festival itself was rained off but the kite has since been flown at many other festivals, including Dieppe 1990 where it was nominated for the 'Best-in-Show' class.

The original design was 4 metres (2½ yards) long and required nearly 18 metres (20 yards) of fabric to make. The version described below is smaller and far less demanding of fabric, but just as much fun.

Materials

Fabric: 8 metres of 40–60 gm (9 yds of 1·25 oz) balloon-quality rip-stop nylon
1·5 metres x 1·5 mm (1¾ yds x ¹⁄₁₆th inch) fibreglass
Rigging: 6 metres (6½ yds) braided polyester/Dacron
Flying line: 80 kg (180 lb) polyester

Construction

1 As this design requires a large amount of fabric and is made up of awkward shapes, start by making paper templates of all the pieces required: back and front (Fig 7·1a and b); use Table 1 (overleaf) to make a template for the outer ribs, from which you can also mark the inner ribs (Fig 7·2a–c); flares (Fig 7·3, overleaf); flukes and flippers (Fig 7·4a and b).

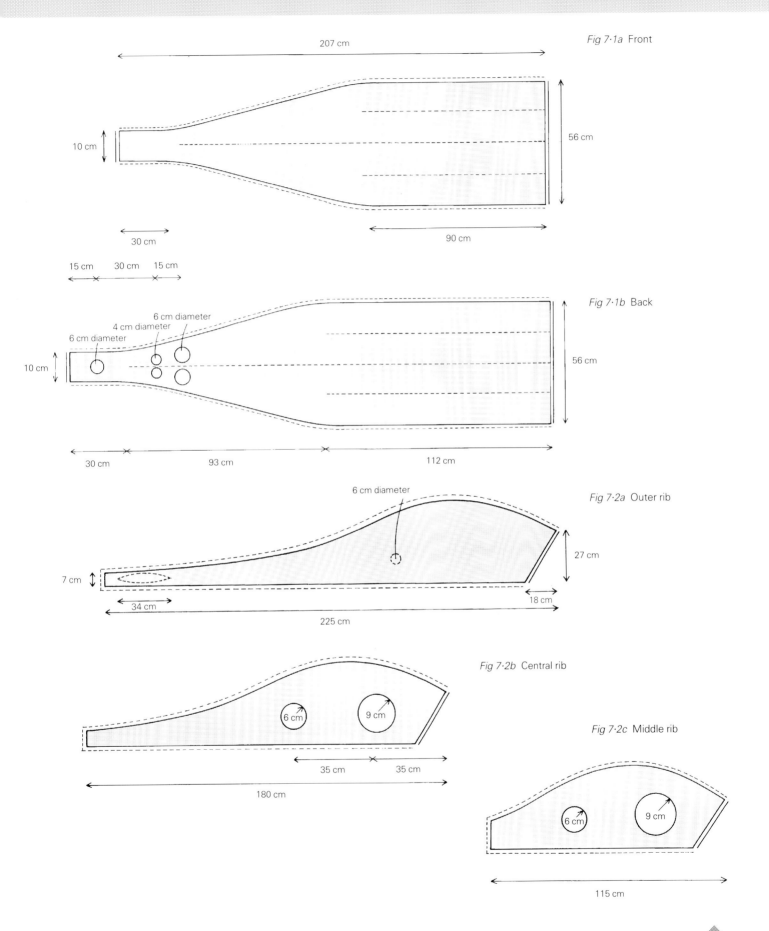

Fig 7·1a Front

207 cm

56 cm

10 cm

30 cm

90 cm

15 cm   30 cm   15 cm

Fig 7·1b Back

6 cm diameter
4 cm diameter
6 cm diameter

10 cm

56 cm

30 cm   93 cm   112 cm

6 cm diameter

Fig 7·2a Outer rib

27 cm

7 cm

34 cm

18 cm

225 cm

Fig 7·2b Central rib

6 cm

9 cm

Fig 7·2c Middle rib

35 cm   35 cm

180 cm

6 cm

9 cm

115 cm

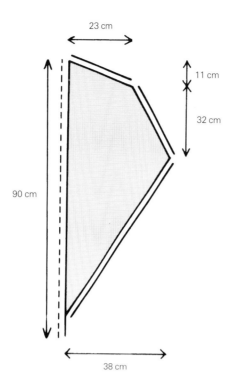

Fig 7·3 Flare

23 cm

11 cm

32 cm

90 cm

38 cm

Table 1: Rib Shape

Distance from leading edge	Height
cm	**cm**
0·0	27·0
5·0	30·0
10·0	33·0
20·0	36·5
30·0	39·0
40·0	40·0
50·0	40·0
60·0	37·0
70·0	33·0
80·0	28·0
90·0	23·0
100·0	20·0
120·0	15·0
140·0	131·0
160·0	11·0
180·0	9·5
200·0	8·0
225·0	7·0

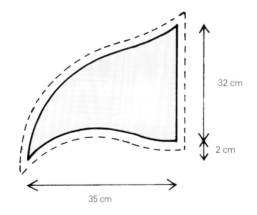

Fig 7·4a Flukes

32 cm

2 cm

35 cm

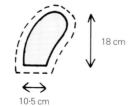

Fig 7·4b Flippers

18 cm

10·5 cm

2 Using the templates mark and cut out the front and back; ribs (2 outer, 2 inner, 1 centre); flares (3); flippers (4); and flukes (4).

3 Bind the forward edges of the flares and sew tape loops to their tips.

4 Hot cut the vents on the back and the inter-cell vents on the inner and central ribs.

5 Cut out suitable scrap pieces of fabric in an alternative colour, and sew them to the outer ribs using the surface-appliqué technique described on pages 22–3 to represent the whale's mouth and eyes.

6 Bind the forward edges of the ribs.

7 Sew the flipper pieces together in pairs, with a seam around the curved edge only. Turn them inside-out, so that the seam edge is on the inside, and sew them to the outer ribs at the position indicated, using a folded seam (Fig 7·5a–c). Cut out a small vent hole in the outer ribs to allow the flippers to inflate.

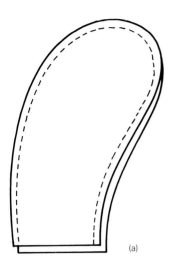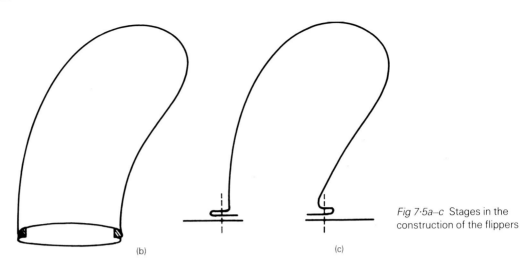

(a)　　　　　(b)　　　　　(c)

Fig 7·5a–c Stages in the construction of the flippers

8　In the same way, sew the flukes together in pairs with seams around the curved edges only. Turn them inside-out and sew a second seam around the convex edge to create a casing to accept the 1·5 mm (¹/₁₆ inch) fibreglass rod. Sew additional seams in a fan pattern to prevent the flukes from inflating too much. Sew a small patch of fabric to reinforce the tips (Fig 7·6).

9　Sew the flukes to the outer ribs in a folded seam and make a small hole in the outer rib, through which you can thread the fibreglass rod (Fig 7·7).

10　The construction now continues in a similar way to standard parafoils. Sew the three inner ribs to the front, then add the flares.

11　Add the outer ribs, and complete the canopy by sewing on the back, using the procedure described with previous designs. Inexperienced kitemakers may come up against the problem of fabric stretch, finding that the back appears not to fit, or is twisted, matching one side but not the other. If there is any mis-match whatsoever, you must undo the seam and start again. If it helps, tape, pin or glue the fabric pieces together before sewing.

Fig 7·6 Construction of the flukes

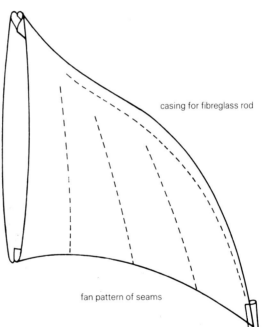

casing for fibreglass rod

fan pattern of seams

fabric-reinforcing patch

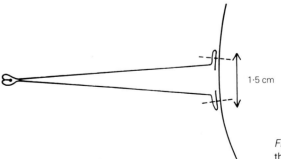

1·5 cm

Fig 7·7 Sew the flukes to the outer ribs

Fig 7·8 Thread a fibreglass rod through the casing in the flukes

fibreglass rod

hole in rib

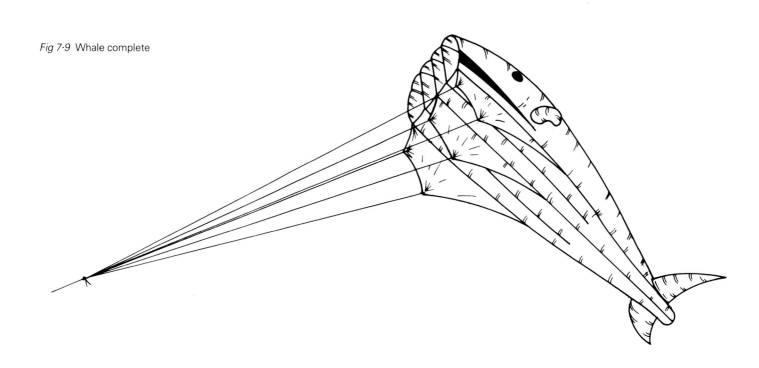

12 Thread a length of 1·5 mm (¹⁄₁₆ inch) fibreglass rod across the body and through the casing on each of the flukes (Fig 7·8).

13 The whale is flat-rigged with line dimensions as shown in Table 2. The finished kite is illustrated in Fig 7·9.

Table 2: Rigging

	2	1	2
A	318 cm	317 cm	318 cm
B	311 cm	310 cm	311 cm

Fig 7·9 Whale complete

FROG

The Frog was designed essentially to be a fun kite and in one respect I suppose I succeeded: it is great fun to fly. The drawback is that its construction is very difficult, and is likely to be a real test of your skills. But don't be put off: if you have successfully built some of the earlier designs, the frog might just be what you are looking for. There are no short cuts, however, so take your time.

Materials

Fabric: 7 metres of 40–60 gm (8 yds of 1·25 oz) balloon-quality rip-stop nylon
Rigging: 20 metres (25 yds) braided polyester
Flying line: 30 kg (70 lb) polyester

Construction

1 As with the whale, you should start by making templates for all the fabric pieces. Use the information from Table 1 to construct the rib template (Fig 7·10) and cut out five pieces of fabric. The central rib has three vent holes; the next-outermost ribs (2 off) will also have three vent holes, but can be trimmed along the lines ZZ^1; the outer ribs (2) will have just two vent holes, towards the trailing edge, and can be trimmed along the lines YY^1.

Table 1: Rib Shape

Distance from leading edge	Upper surface	Lower surface
cm	cm	cm
5·0	19·0	
10·0	21·5	2·0
15·0	23·0	1·5
20·0	24·0	1·0
25·0	24·0	0·0
30·0	24·5	
35·0	25·0	
40·0	26·0	
50·0	27·5	
60·0	28·5	
65·0	29·0	
70·0	28·0	
80·0	24·5	
90·0	18·0	
100·0	10·0	
102·0	0·0	

2 Cut out the back and front (Fig 7·11a and b, overleaf). It is easier to mark the positions of the line-attachment points at this stage rather than when the kite is constructed (Fig 7·12).

3 Cut out two of each of the outer-body panels (Fig 7·13a and b). The length of the curved edges on these pieces should be checked against the rib. Because of slight puckering which will occur during

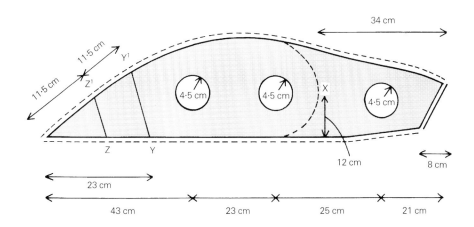

Fig 7·10 Rib

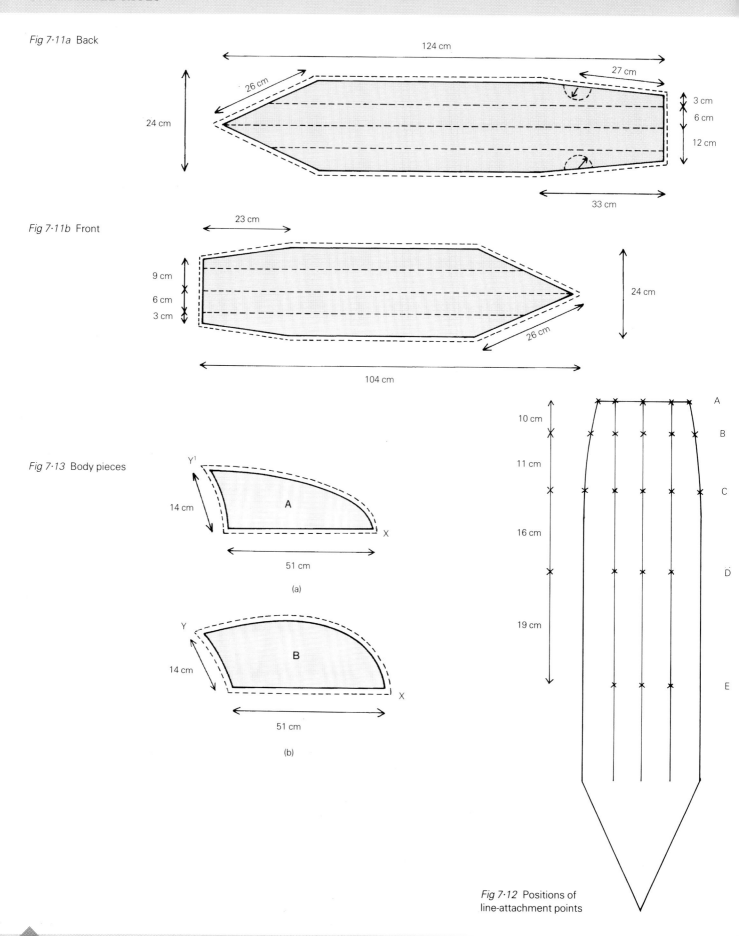

Fig 7·11a Back

124 cm

26 cm

27 cm

24 cm

3 cm
6 cm
12 cm

33 cm

Fig 7·11b Front

23 cm

9 cm
6 cm
3 cm

24 cm

26 cm

104 cm

Fig 7·13 Body pieces

Y¹

14 cm

A

X

51 cm

(a)

Y

14 cm

B

X

51 cm

(b)

10 cm
11 cm
16 cm
19 cm

A
B
C
D
E

Fig 7·12 Positions of line-attachment points

sewing, the curved edges on the body pieces should be about 0·5 cm (¼ inch) longer than the rib contour. Piece A should fit from point X around the lower contour to point Y; piece B should fit around the upper contour of the rib to point Y¹.

4 Cut out four leg pieces (Fig 7·14) and two of each of the eye pieces (Fig 7·15a and b).

5 To make the eyes, sew the pieces together in pairs, with a plain seam around the curved edge. Turn them inside-out and sew to the edge of the back at the positions shown (Fig 7·16).

6 Join the outer-body pieces together in pairs, with a seam along the straight edge. Position the junction of the two pieces at point X and sew them, using a folded seam, to the outer ribs: piece A along the lower contour of the ribs and B along the upper contour (Fig 7·17a and b, overleaf).

7 Sew the ribs in position following a procedure similar to the standard parafoil (see page 36). Add the back. Make a small hole in the back to allow the eyes to inflate.

8 Join the leg pieces together in pairs with a seam around the perimeter, leaving a gap (Fig 7·18). Turn the legs inside-out.

9 Join the legs to the body (Fig 7·19). This is the most difficult stage, and, depending on how accurately you have cut and sewn the pieces, some slight adjustments may be necessary.

10 Complete the seam on the inside of the legs to close the rear edge of the kite (Fig 7·20).

11 Sew the legs together with a short seam at the feet (ankle joint).

12 Add the rigging lines. These should be attached to the body, not with tapes as in previous designs, but threaded to the appropriate points using a large darning needle, and tied in a half-blood or similar knot (Fig 7·21).

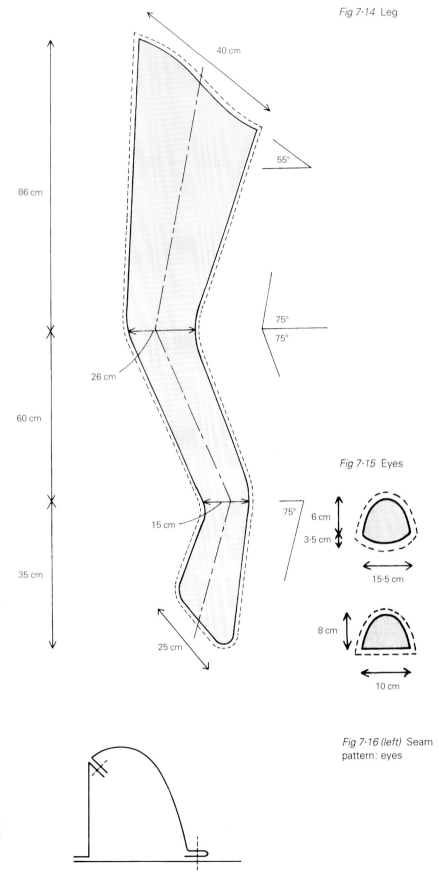

Fig 7·14 Leg

Fig 7·15 Eyes

Fig 7·16 (left) Seam pattern: eyes

Fig 7·17a Sew the body
pieces to the outer ribs

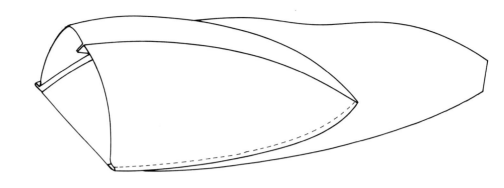

Fig 7·17b Seam pattern:
body pieces

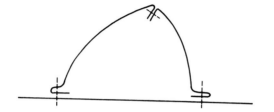

Fig 7·18 Join the leg
pieces together in pairs,
leaving a gap in the
stitching

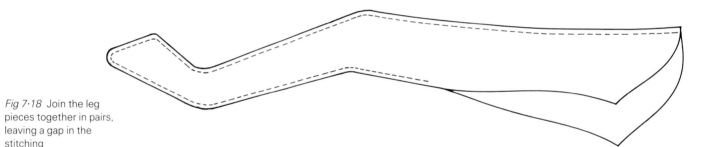

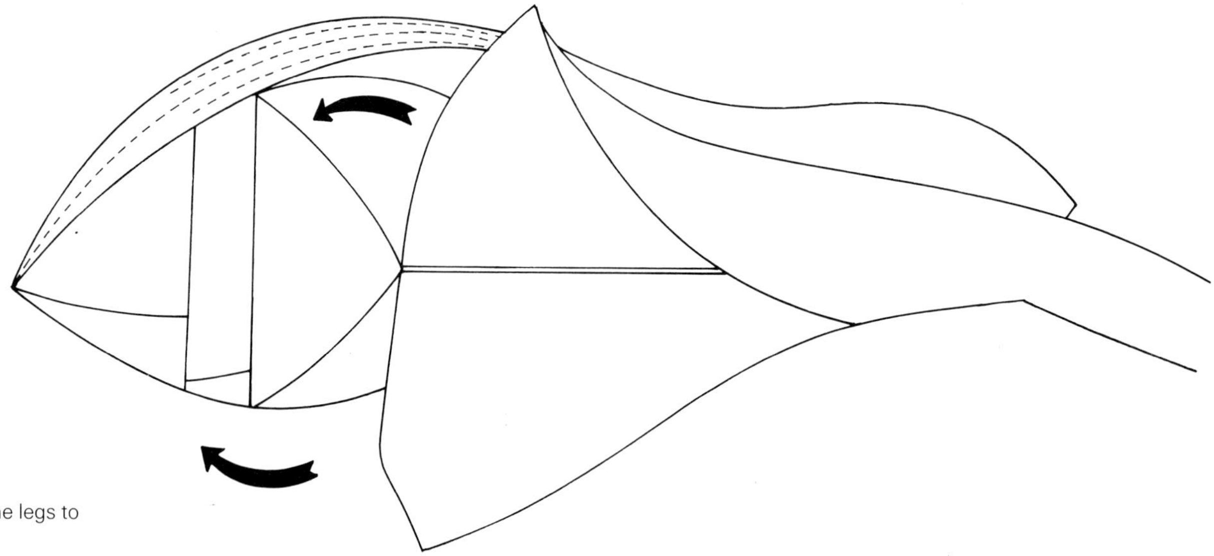

Fig 7·19 Join the legs to
the body

13 Lines should be attached in pairs to positions on opposite sides: left-hand A1 to right-hand A1, and so on. As with previous designs, cut lines slightly shorter than shown in Table 2. Tie overhand loops at their centres and the loose ends to the kite. Collect the set of lines together, with an additional short length of line to provide a suitable towing point (Fig 7·22).

Table 2: Rigging

A	143 cm
B	142 cm
C	142 cm
D	145 cm
E	154 cm

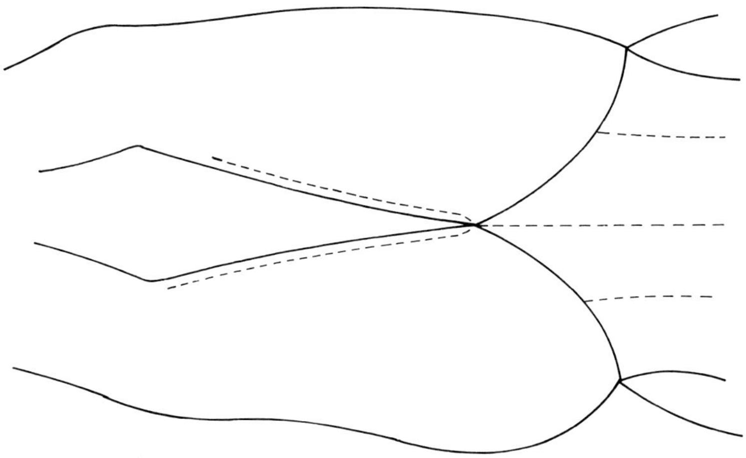

Fig 7·20 Complete the seams on the inner junctions of the leg pieces

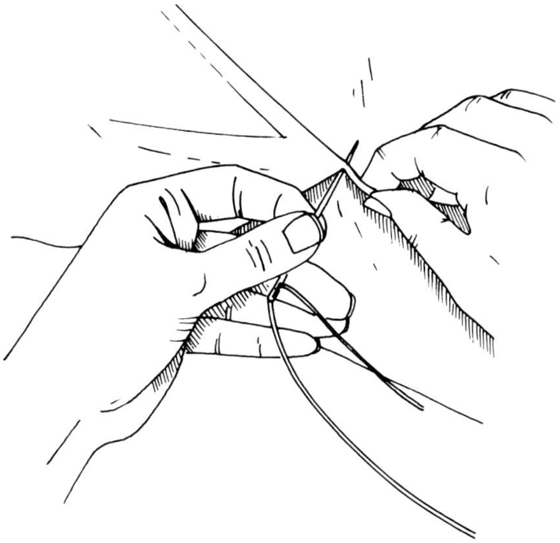

Fig 7·21 Attach the lines directly to the body, threading them through the fabric layers with a darning needle

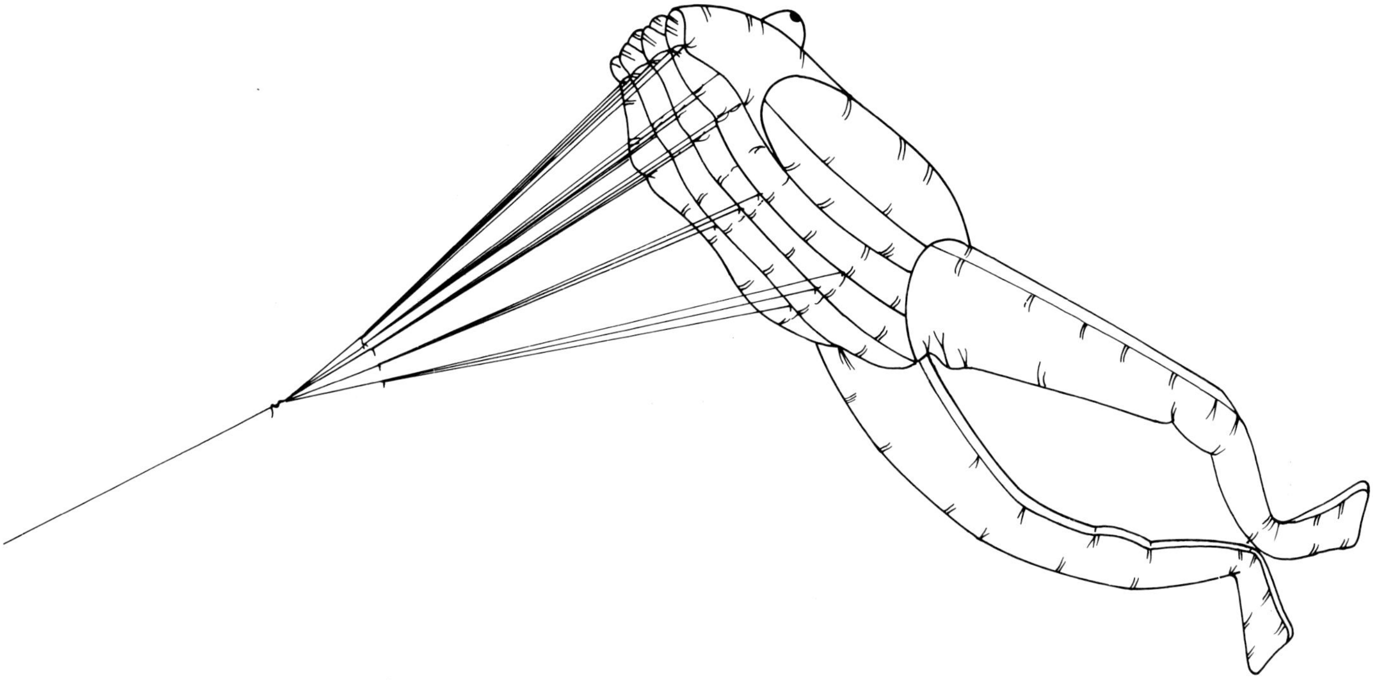

Fig 7·22 Frog complete

Windsocks

BASIC CYLINDER WINDSOCK

The simplest windsock is constructed in the shape of a long cone. The dimensions shown in the illustrations are merely by way of example, and windsocks of this type can be made to almost any combination of length, diameter and taper. The only rule to bear in mind is that, to achieve good inflation, the diameter of the narrower opening should be no more than two-thirds of the wider one. A gentle taper, making the windsock length 5 to 7 times the wider diameter, is also suggested.

Materials

Fabric: 2 metres (2¼ yds) rip-stop nylon or taffeta in a range of colours
Tie lines: 3 metres (3 yds) braided polyester

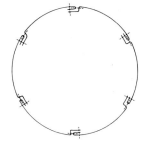

Fig 8·2 Seam pattern: make a cylinder using a plain or folded seam

Fig 8·1 Fabric pattern

Construction

1 Mark and cut out six pieces of fabric (Fig 8·1).

2 Sew them together along the edges AC to make up a cylinder (Fig 8·2). A folded seam makes a neater finish than a plain seam.

3 Bind or hem the edges top and bottom.

4 Sew six tape loops evenly around the edge at the wider opening (Fig 8·3).

5 The tie lines are probably best fitted in pairs. Cut three lines approximately three times the greater diameter in length, and tie an overhand loop at their centres. Tie the loose ends to the tape loops and adjust the lines so that they are all the same length. Collect the loops together with a single line (Fig 8·4).

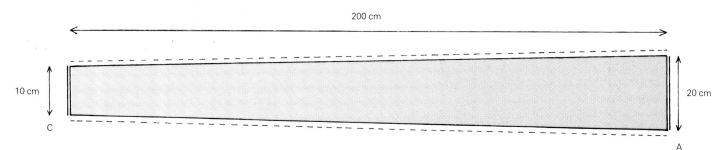

200 cm

10 cm

C

20 cm

A

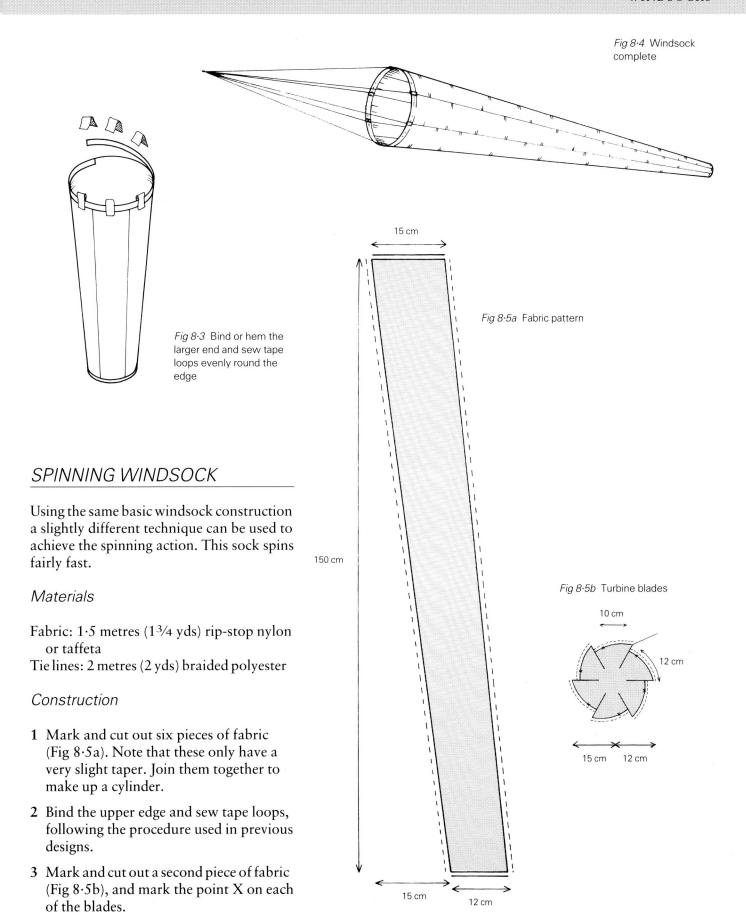

Fig 8·4 Windsock complete

Fig 8·3 Bind or hem the larger end and sew tape loops evenly round the edge

Fig 8·5a Fabric pattern

15 cm

150 cm

15 cm

12 cm

Fig 8·5b Turbine blades

10 cm

12 cm

15 cm   12 cm

SPINNING WINDSOCK

Using the same basic windsock construction a slightly different technique can be used to achieve the spinning action. This sock spins fairly fast.

Materials

Fabric: 1·5 metres (1¾ yds) rip-stop nylon
   or taffeta
Tie lines: 2 metres (2 yds) braided polyester

Construction

1 Mark and cut out six pieces of fabric (Fig 8·5a). Note that these only have a very slight taper. Join them together to make up a cylinder.

2 Bind the upper edge and sew tape loops, following the procedure used in previous designs.

3 Mark and cut out a second piece of fabric (Fig 8·5b), and mark the point X on each of the blades.

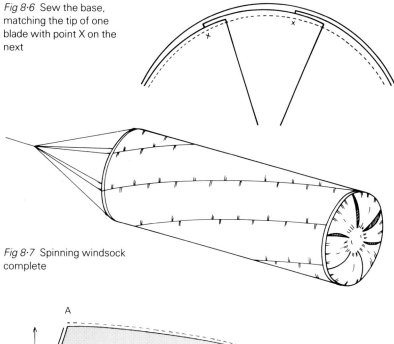

Fig 8·6 Sew the base, matching the tip of one blade with point X on the next

Fig 8·7 Spinning windsock complete

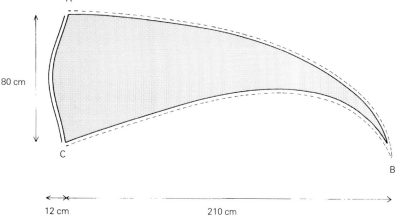

A

80 cm

C

B

12 cm   210 cm

Fig 8·8 Fabric pattern

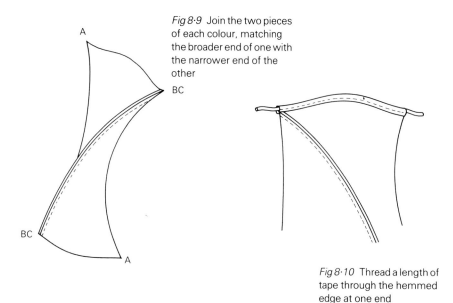

A

BC

Fig 8·9 Join the two pieces of each colour, matching the broader end of one with the narrower end of the other

BC

A

Fig 8·10 Thread a length of tape through the hemmed edge at one end

4 Turn the windsock inside-out, and with the seam edges on the outside, sew the blades to the narrower end, matching the tip of one blade with the point X of its neighbour (Fig 8·6).

5 To achieve the spinning action, it should be tied to the supporting line via 2–3 swivels in series (Fig 8·7).

RASPBERRY TWIST

In flight the Raspberry Twist resembles two cylinders, or snakes, entwined around each other, which revolve very slowly and gently. It is rather excessive on fabric, and it is therefore probably better to make up each of the basic sections from a number of pieces of fabric.

Materials

Fabric: 7·5 metres (8 yds) balloon-quality rip-stop nylon or taffeta
Tie lines: 3 metres (3 yds) braided polyester

Construction

1 Make a template using the information given in Table 1 and Fig 8·8 and cut out two pieces from each of two colours of fabric.

2 For each colour, sew the two pieces together, matching the broader end of one with the pointed end of the other, along the edge BC (Fig 8·9).

3 Bind both edges AB with a broad tape and, through one, thread some thick line or fabric tape (Fig 8·10).

4 Join the two colours together by folding the seam edges and re-sewing along the previous seam line. Leave a short gap in the stitching of about 8 cm (3⅛ inches) towards the lower end (Fig 8·11).

Table 1: Template Shape

Distance from forward (left-hand) edge	Height of upper curve	Height of lower curve
cm	cm	cm
0·0	80·0	0·0
20·0	79·5	7·0
40·0	78·5	13·5
60·0	76·5	19·5
80·0	74·0	24·5
100·0	70·0	28·5
120·0	65·5	31·5
130·0	63·0	32·5
140·0	59·5	33·0
150·0	56·0	33·0
160·0	51·0	33·0
170·0	47·0	32·0
180·0	41·0	30·0
190·0	34·0	26·5
195·0	29·5	23·5
200·0	24·5	20·5
205·0	17·0	15·5
210·0	0·0	0·0

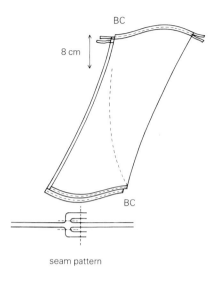

Fig 8·11 Re-stitch along the line BC to join the two tubes together

seam pattern

5 To complete each tube, wrap the pieces of one colour around to enclose the other, then bring the loose edges together and sew a plain seam. Turn the tube inside-out and repeat with the other colour (Fig 8·12a and b).

6 With the two tubes completed, sew tape loops evenly around the openings and add tie lines as in previous windsocks. At the other end, use the drawstring to partially close the end of the tube (Fig 8·13).

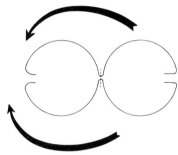

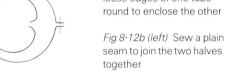

Fig 8·12a (above) Fold the loose edges of one tube round to enclose the other

Fig 8·12b (left) Sew a plain seam to join the two halves together

Footnote

For those with knowledge of mathematics and access to a computer, the dimensions of this windsock can be altered using the formulae below:

Upper curve: $y_1 = a * sqrt(1 - (x/b)^2)$

Lower curve: $y_2 = y_1 - b + (a/b) * x$

where x represents points on the horizontal axis, and y represents points on the vertical axis. 'a' is the circumference of each tube, and 'b' the length.

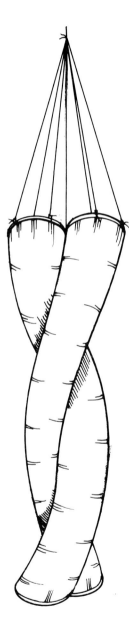

Fig 8·13 Raspberry Twist complete

Fig 8·14 Caterpillar pattern

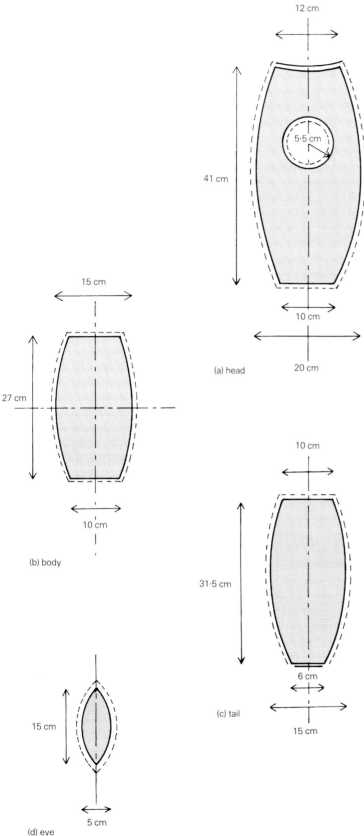

(a) head

(b) body

(c) tail

(d) eye

CATERPILLAR

The caterpillar is a relatively simple windsock, time-consuming to make but interesting to fly. In the past, I have noticed that younger children especially seem fascinated by its shape, and how it wriggles in the sky.

Materials

Fabric: 3·5 metres (4 yds) balloon-quality rip-stop nylon
Tie lines: 2 metres (2¼ yds) braided polyester

Construction

1   Make templates for each of the body shapes (Fig 8·14a–d). Cut out the head, 6 pieces; the body, 60 pieces; and the tail, 6 pieces. Number the head pieces 1–6 and mark the eye position (shown by the circle in Fig 8·14a) on numbers 1 and 2. Do not cut the eye vents yet.

2   Cut out an additional 6 pieces of fabric (Fig 8·14d) for the eyes. To make the eyes, sew these pieces together in two groups of three to create a hemisphere, and then sew them to the two head pieces, making a neat seam (Fig 8·15). Cut out the holes on the head pieces to allow the eyes to inflate.

3   Join the head sections together in sequence to complete the cylinder.

4   Next make up each body segment individually. Sew the six pieces together to make up the cylinder, then sew it to its neighbour. If your sewing machine has a sleeve arm you will find it very useful here. Finally, add the tail and head (Fig 8·16).

5   At the head, bind the open edges and sew short tape loops evenly around the edges.

6   Tie lines to the loops, adjusted so that each is 30 cm (12 inches) long (Fig 8·17).

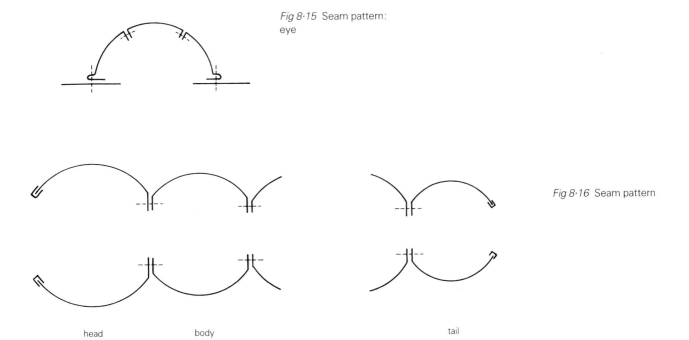

Fig 8·15 Seam pattern:
eye

Fig 8·16 Seam pattern

head   body   tail

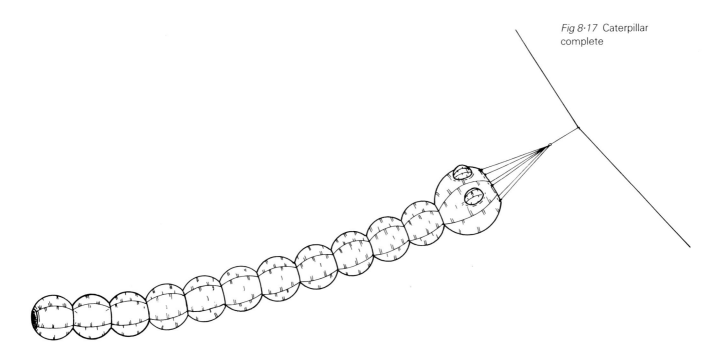

Fig 8·17 Caterpillar
complete

Fig 8·18 Soldier pattern

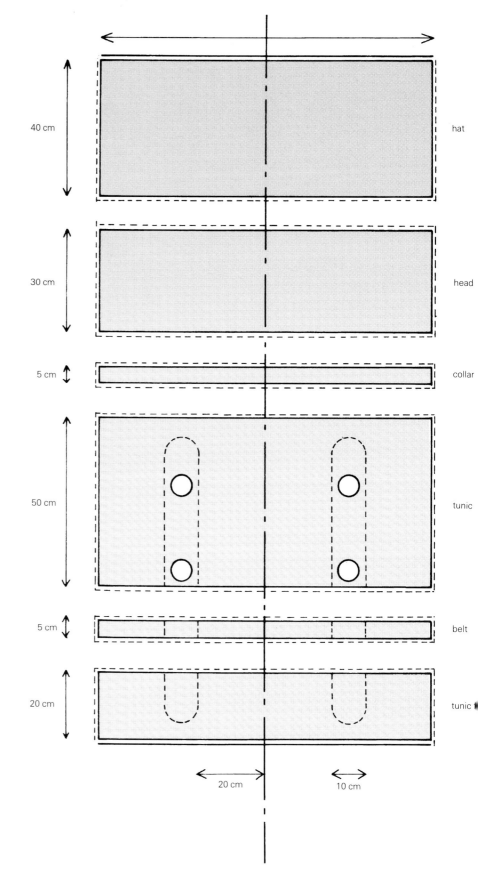

40 cm — hat

30 cm — head

5 cm — collar

50 cm — tunic

5 cm — belt

20 cm — tunic

20 cm   10 cm

Fig 8·19 Arm pieces

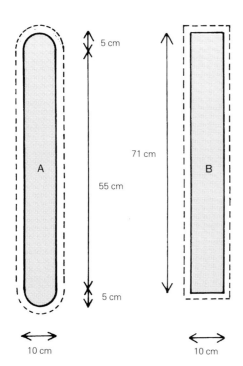

5 cm

71 cm

55 cm

5 cm

A   B

10 cm   10 cm

SOLDIER

This design was based on a sketch by Eddie Megrath. The construction is not particularly difficult, but creating the actual design, using appliqué, colour combinations of fabric and, in some instances, embroidery, can be demanding and time-consuming.

The design shown here is for the guardsman standing to attention, but there is no reason why other characters cannot be created using different colours and shapes.

Materials

Fabric: 4 metres (4 ½ yds) rip-stop nylon in various colours (see below)
Tie lines: 2 metres (2 ¼ yds) braided polyester
1·25 metres x 2 mm (55 inches x ³/₃₂ inch) fibreglass

Construction

Suggested colour scheme:

Hat   – black
Tunic   – red
Face   – flesh-pink or white with appliqué for nose and eyes
Collar   – black and gold
Arms   – red, with white for gloves
Belt   – gold or yellow
Trousers – black

Head and Hat

1 Cut out rectangular pieces of fabric for the head and hat (Fig 8·18). Select additional coloured pieces of fabric to create a suitable design for the face, chinstrap and hair, and appliqué them to the head (see page 22).

2 Sew the two pieces (head and hat) together.

Tunic

3 Cut out the rectangular pieces which make up the collar, tunic body, tunic flap and belt (Fig 8·18). Mark, but do not cut the vent holes for the arms yet.

4 Join the collar, tunic body and belt together.

5 Bind or hem the lower edge of the tunic flap and sew to the completed body piece. Here you should use a plain seam leaving a good excess of fabric to create a lip. The reasons for this will become clearer later.

6 Cut out the pieces to make up the arms: four of piece A and two of piece B (Fig 8·19). Join two of the A pieces end-on-end to make a hoop, and sew them around the perimeter of piece B. Sew the arms to the body along the lines marked using a welted seam (Fig 8·20a and b). Cut out the arm-vent holes.

7 Join the head and hat to the body, then sew the sides together to make up a cylinder.

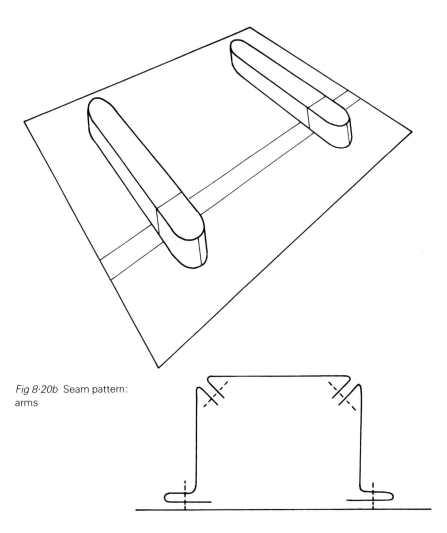

Fig 8·20a Sew the arms to the tunic

Fig 8·20b Seam pattern: arms

Fig 8·21 Trousers

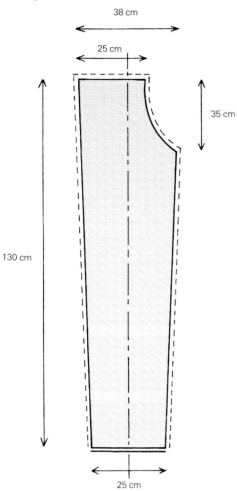

38 cm

25 cm

35 cm

130 cm

25 cm

Legs

8 Cut out four pieces of fabric (Fig 8·21). Bind or hem the bottom edges as shown.

9 Join them together in pairs with a single seam around the curved edge (Fig 8·22).

10 Open each leg out, and lay them flat, with the right side inside. Sew them together along the straight edges (Fig 8·23).

Fig 8·22 Sew a plain seam along the curved edge

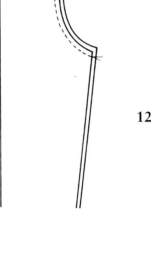

To complete the windsock

11 Turn the body inside-out, folded at the junction of the tunic flap and the waistband. Thread the legs inside the cylinder and sew them to the body, along the same seam line as that between the tunic flap and the waistband. The body should be wrong-side out, the legs and tunic flap right-side out (Fig 8·24).

12 Turn the body section the right way round to make the windsock erect, and bind the larger (head) opening with a broad tape. Sew six tape loops at equal intervals around the edge and tie suitable lines (Fig 8·25). Thread the fibreglass through the hem so formed.

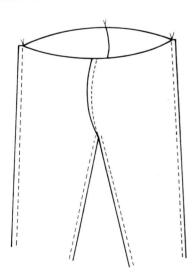

Fig 8·23 Complete the trousers with a seam along the straight edges

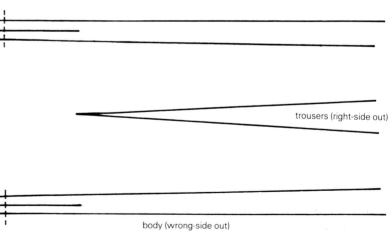

trousers (right-side out)

body (wrong-side out)

Fig 8·24 Seam pattern: join the trousers to the body with a seam along the junction between the tunic flap and the belt

Fig 8·25 Soldier complete

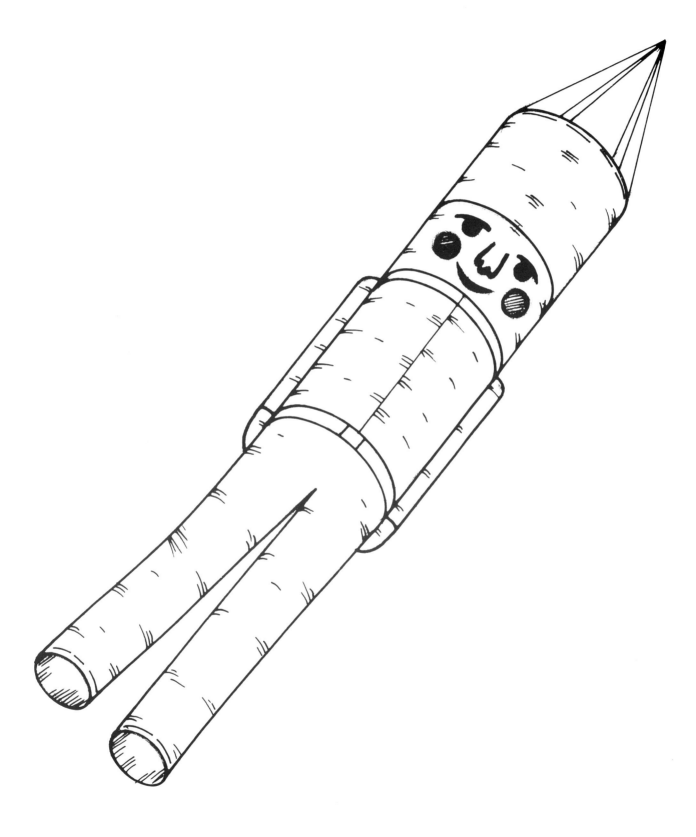

9

Drogues

Like framed kites, parafoils and inflatables sometimes need a little help to maintain stability in gusty wind conditions. However, as these designs are generally much lighter than similar-sized framed kites, the traditional tail with tasselled edges may be too heavy, pulling it into stall without necessarily increasing stability. Parafoils and inflatables therefore tend to use an alternative lightweight stabilizing device called a drogue.

A drogue is rather like a small windsock: a cone shape, constructed from a number of pieces of fabric. It acts in the same way as a tail, adding a small amount of drag, and, like a long rudder or pendulum, dampens yawing oscillations. To achieve the desired stability the size of the drogue must, however, be balanced to the size of the kite. Large drogues may add too much drag and pull the kite beyond stall, preventing lift; or, at the other extreme, small drogues may not dampen motions sufficiently.

Unfortunately there are no universally understood terms to describe the size of a drogue. Large, small and medium are used but these are of course relative and not altogether helpful. Nor is consideration of the aerodynamics of any greater assistance. The amount of drag generated by the drogue is dependent not only on the size of the larger opening but also on its ratio to the narrower one. But as a very approximate guide, the larger diameter of the drogue should be approximately one-tenth of the kite's span, and the smaller diameter 50 per cent of the larger one.

Drogues are usually attached to the trailing edges of the kite via either a single line to the centre, or in a Y shape, with the two upper legs tied at the lower corners (Fig 9·1a and b).

Consideration of simple dynamics would suggest that the length of these lines should be a non-harmonic multiple of the chord length. That is, they should be five, seven, or eleven times the length of the chord, not two, three or four. This will ensure that the drogue dampens oscillations rather than enhancing them. My own preference is for lines around seven times the chord length, although, as with much in kite design, this is by no means a hard-and-fast rule.

STANDARD DROGUE

A simple drogue can be made from four pieces of fabric from the scrap box. As with all the drogue designs featured, dimensions can be scaled up or down to suit a particular type of kite.

Materials

Fabric: 0·25 metre (15 inches) rip-stop
nylon or nylon taffeta
Tie lines: 1 metre (1 yd) braided polyester

Construction

1 Cut out four pieces of fabric (Fig 9·2).

2 Sew them together to create the cone,
either using a plain seam, or the much
neater folded seam.

3 Bind or hem the larger open edge
(Fig 9·3).

4 Sew tape loops evenly around this edge.

5 Make up two lengths of line and tie
overhand loops at their centres. Tie each
of the loose ends to the tape ties and
adjust them to the required lengths
(approximately one-and-a-half times the
larger diameter). Join the loops together
with a third length of line (Fig 9·4).

Fig 9·1 Alternative
methods of attaching
drogue lines to the trailing
edge of the kite

single line to centre

Y form

(a)

(b)

Fig 9·3 (below) Bind or
hem the large end and sew
tape loops round the
circumference

Fig 9·2 Fabric pattern

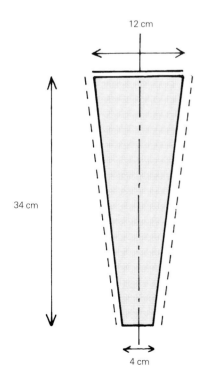

12 cm

34 cm

4 cm

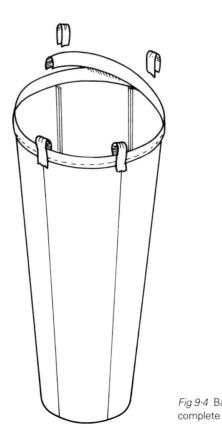

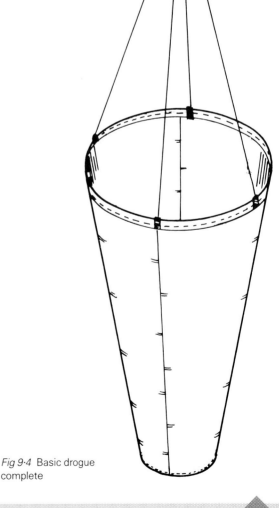

Fig 9·4 Basic drogue
complete

VARIABLE-DRAG DROGUE

To be able to use the same drogue in a range of wind conditions and on a number of different kites, it is often useful to be able to vary the drag that it imposes. You can do this by adding a drawstring to the narrower end of the drogue, and altering it to increase or decrease the diameter.

Materials

Fabric: 0·25 metre (15 inches) rip-stop nylon or nylon taffeta
Tie lines: 1·5 metres (1¾ yds) braided polyester

Construction

1 Cut out four pieces of fabric (Fig 9·5). Notice that the taper on these is less sharp than on the standard drogue.

2 Sew them together to create a cone and bind the larger end as above.

3 Sew a broad hem to the lower edge (Fig 9·6), leaving a small gap.

4 Thread a narrow tape through the lower hem to vary the size of the opening.

5 Add four lines as described with the standard drogue (Fig 9·7).

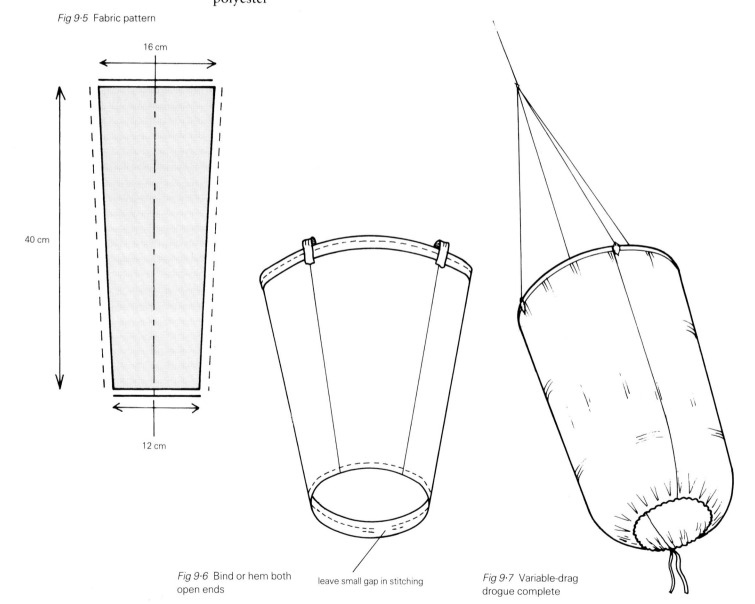

Fig 9·5 Fabric pattern

16 cm

40 cm

12 cm

Fig 9·6 Bind or hem both open ends

leave small gap in stitching

Fig 9·7 Variable-drag drogue complete

PUMPKIN DROGUE

The pumpkin is a simple sculpted drogue, which is also used as the base for the caterpillar described on page 76.

Materials

Fabric: 0·25 metre (15 inches) rip-stop nylon or nylon taffeta
Tie lines: 1·5 metres (1¾ yds) braided polyester

Construction

1 Cut out six pieces of fabric in a range of colours (Fig 9·8).

2 Sew the pieces together to make up a ball, following the procedure used in previous designs.

3 Bind or hem both edges, and sew or glue long, narrow ribbons of scrap fabric around the rim of the smaller opening.

4 Sew six tape loops evenly around the larger opening and tie lines as described on page 83 (Fig 9·9).

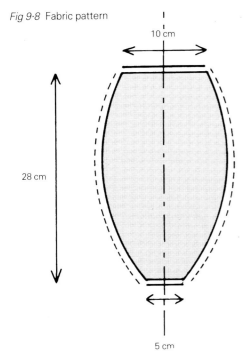

Fig 9·8 Fabric pattern

10 cm

28 cm

5 cm

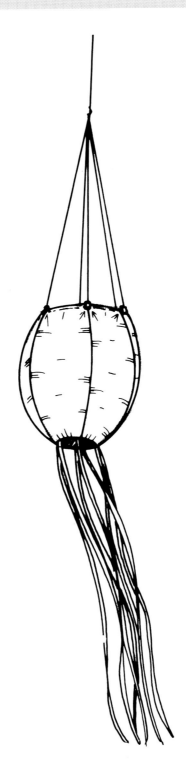

Fig 9·9 Pumpkin drogue complete

WINGED DROGUE

A variation on the standard drogue which shares a similar construction.

Materials

Fabric: 0·25 metre (15 inches) rip-stop nylon or nylon taffeta

Tie lines: 1·5 metres (1¾ yds) braided polyester

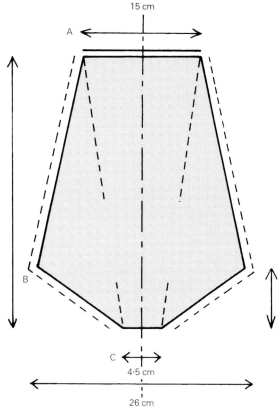

Fig 9·10 Fabric pattern

Construction

1 Mark and cut out four pieces of fabric (Fig 9·10) and bind the edges as marked.

2 Sew them together along the edges AB to make up a box shape. To achieve the desired wing shape you should sew a French seam (see Fig 2·9b on page 20).

3 Sew a row of stitches along the lines AC to join each face of the box to its neighbour, leaving a break of perhaps 6–8 cm near the lower end.

4 Sew four tape loops evenly around the open edge and tie lines in a similar fashion to previous designs (Fig 9·11).

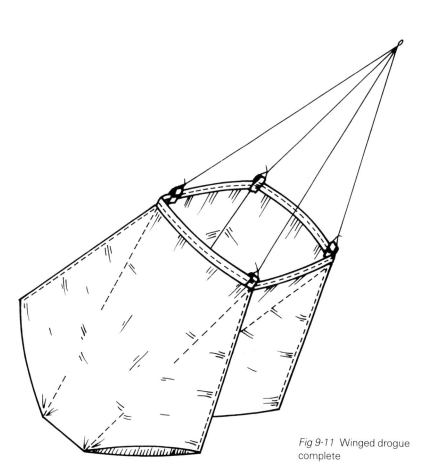

Fig 9·11 Winged drogue complete

DIABLO DROGUE

This is a slightly different spinning drogue. It has the advantage of not requiring a fibreglass hoop to keep it in shape.

Materials

Fabric: 0·5 metre (20 inches) rip-stop nylon

Tie lines: 1·5 metres (1¾ yds) braided polyester

Construction

1 Cut out six pieces of fabric (Fig 9·12a) in a range of colours. Cut out the second section (Fig 9·12b).

2 Sew the six pieces together to make up the cylinder. Bind one edge and sew six evenly spaced tape loops around the circumference, as in previous designs.

3 Fold the cylinder inside-out, so that the seam edges are on the outside and mark two diametrically opposite points X and X^1. Line up the point X with a similar point X on fabric piece B and sew towards point Y. Similarly, match up point X^1 and sew towards Y^1. Now return to X and X^1 and sew in the opposite direction to complete the seams.

4 Turn the drogue the right way out and tie lines as in previous designs. Normally drogues can be tied to their accompanying lines with just a single swivel. With spinning drogues or windsocks it is probably better to use 2 or 3 swivels (Fig 9·13).

5 The speed of this particular drogue can be changed by altering the size of the vent holes on piece B.

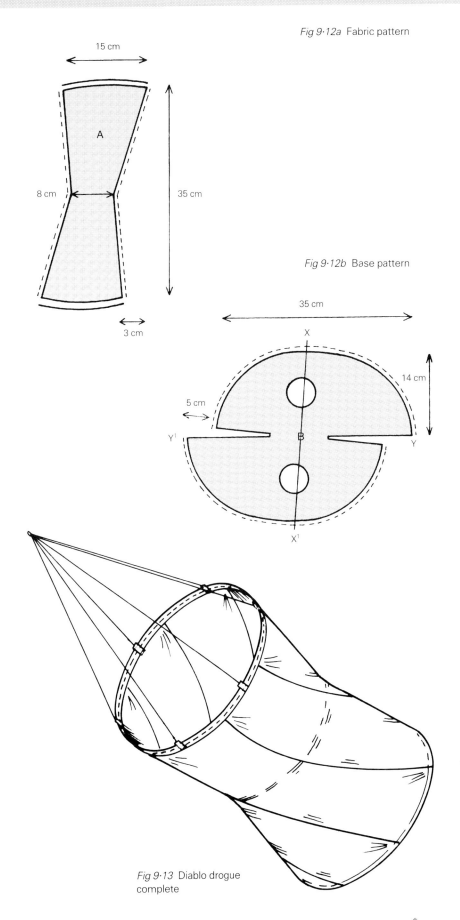

Fig 9·12a Fabric pattern

Fig 9·12b Base pattern

Fig 9·13 Diablo drogue complete

Fig 10·1 Single-handed launch

10

Flying and looking after your Kites

Having built your kite, the next step is obviously to take it into the wind and give it a good test flight. For this you should choose a lighter wind (8–10 mph) and be prepared to make some adjustments.

As soft kites cannot be positioned into the wind like framed kites, techniques for launching are slightly different.

SINGLE-HANDED LAUNCH

To achieve a single-handed launch, lay the kite flat on its back, and, in one hand, take hold of the lines slightly forward of the convergence point. Take hold of the secondary A line with the other hand and, tugging it, lift the kite into the air. As the kite inflates and starts to rise let go of the A line and start to feed the flying line. If one or two cells have not inflated fully (usually the outer ones) give a few hard tugs on the flying line (Fig 10·1).

LADDER LAUNCH

The ladder launch is more suited to large parafoils which are anchored rather than hand-held. Anchor the kite, and unwind the intended length of line. Move the kite to its maximum position downwind from the anchor and approximately 30 degrees from the wind direction.

Lay the kite on one side, rib to the ground. With one hand near the convergence point, use the outermost A line to lift the kite off the ground. As the outermost cell inflates, lift the next one, then the next, and so on (Fig 10·2a and b, overleaf).

As the final cells are inflating, the kite will start to turn to its upright position and the line tension will begin to increase. This is your cue to get out of the way, moving back along the flying line, but still keeping hold of it at this stage to guide the ascent.

KITE STORAGE AND TRANSPORT

If they are not stored properly, the large number of lines on soft kites can become tangled, creating difficulties when you next come to fly them. Tying the lines and re-folding the kite carefully is therefore more important than with framed kites, and the procedure should become second nature.

After detaching the flying line from the rigging the first stage is to disconnect the drogue and to wind the line neatly around a

(a)

(b)

Fig 10·2 Ladder launch

small former. The rigging lines should then be collected together and tied in a procedure somewhat akin to knitting.

1 Collect the rigging lines together and make a single loop towards the kite end (Fig 10·3a).

2 Putting your hand through the loop, take hold of the lower part of the line and pull it through to make a second loop (Fig 10·3b). Pull on the knot you have made to make it tight (Fig 10·3c). Repeat this until you have conveniently tied the lines (Fig 10·3d). This knot is easy to untie. Simply pull on the line at the towing point and it should come apart.

3 To fold the kite for storage, lay it flat, with the back to the ground, and fold the outer edges towards the centre. Repeat this a second and a third time if necessary. Now roll the kite, with the top and bottom to the middle, and place it neatly, together with the drogue, in the storage bag (Fig 10·4a–d). As with framed kites, it is not a good idea to roll the kite up from one side.

Fig 10·3a (left) Bring the rigging lines together and make a single loop

Fig 10·3b (right) Bring upper part of line through loop to make a second loop

Fig 10·3c (left) Pull knot so formed tight and continue in the same way

Fig 10·3d (right) Rigging lines neatly tied

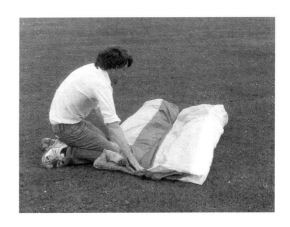

Fig 10·4a (left) Lay the kite flat on its back

Fig 10·4b (right) Fold it to the centre, then fold once more

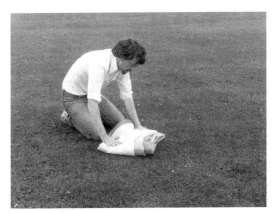

Fig 10·4c (left) Fold it to the centre in the opposite direction

Fig 10·4d (right) Kite neatly folded away and ready to fit into storage bag

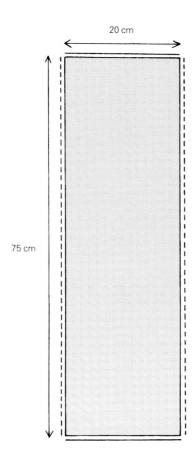

Fig 10·5 Fabric pattern

20 cm

75 cm

KITE BAGS

To keep the kite clean, neat and out of the way it will help to have some sort of permanent storage bag. There are two types of construction techniques which may be used to make such a bag.

Envelope bag

This is more suitable for windsocks and smaller sleds and parafoils which will fold flat.

1 To estimate the size of bag required, fold the kite as described above and measure its final size, length and diameter.

2 Cut a long rectangle of fabric as shown in Fig 10·5. Bind or hem the edges, fold it to the required dimensions, and sew around the edge. Also include a short length of fabric tape (Fig 10·6).

3 Unfold the bag, put the kite inside and bring the loose edge under the tape (Fig 10·7).

Fig 10·6 Fold and sew the fabric, enclosing a short length of tape

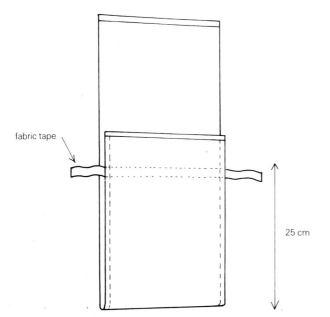

fabric tape

25 cm

Fig 10·7 Envelope bag complete

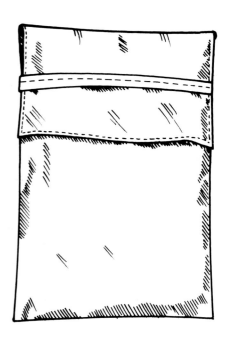

Drawstring bag

1 Again, assess the size of bag required from the dimensions of the folded kite.

2 Mark and cut a circle of fabric to the intended diameter (Fig 10·8a). Cut a rectangular piece of fabric, of a length 3·2 times the diameter of the circle (Fig 10·8b).

3 Make a deep hem, about 1·5 cm (¾ inch) wide, along the edge of the rectangular piece. Fold it along the centre line and sew a seam to join the loose edges, creating a cylinder (Fig 10·9).

4 Sew both pieces together around the circumference of the circle.

5 Thread some broad kite line, string or fabric tape through the hem to complete the bag (Fig 10·10).

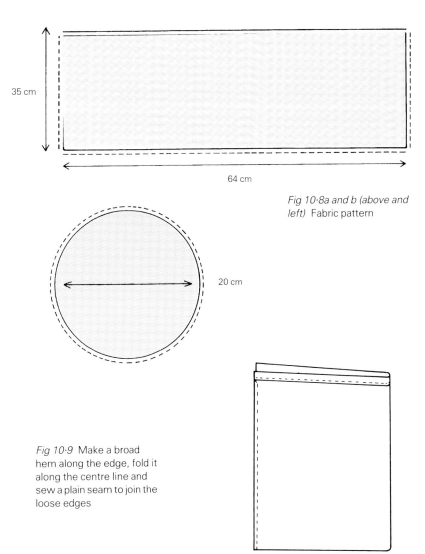

35 cm

64 cm

Fig 10·8a and b (above and left) Fabric pattern

20 cm

Fig 10·9 Make a broad hem along the edge, fold it along the centre line and sew a plain seam to join the loose edges

CARING FOR YOUR KITES

Kites which have been flown in damp or dusty air, or have been dragged along wet grass or sand, are apt to get very dirty and extremely smelly, not only spoiling their colour but also making their handling unpleasant. After each flight, as well as checking them for minor repairs, their overall condition should also be considered.

Rip-stop nylon can be washed in a very mild detergent at low temperatures, then rinsed well and either spun or hung dried. Never iron your kites.

If you follow the above procedures, your kite should last to provide as much fun and pleasure as you wish, for as long as you wish.

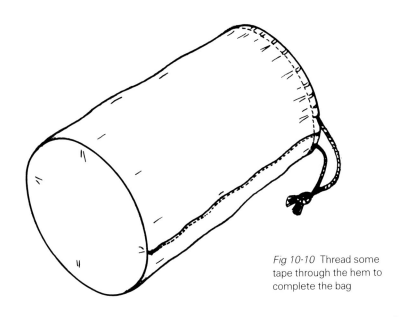

Fig 10·10 Thread some tape through the hem to complete the bag

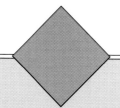

Bibliography

The following items have been used as sources of reference:

ABBOTT, I. H AND VON DOENHOFF, A.E *Theory of wing sections*, Dover, 1958

BURK, S.M AND WARE, G.M 'Static aerodynamic characteristics of three low-aspect-ratio ram-air inflated wings' *NASA* TN-D-4182, Sept. 1967

DENNIS, D.R 'Recent advances in parachute technology' *Aeronautical Journal*, 87, Nov. 1983, pp. 333–342

GOODRICK, T.F 'Scale effects on the performance of ram-air wings', 8th Aerodynamic Decelerator and Balloon Technology Conference, Hyannis, Montana, USA, April 1984; New York, AIAA 1984; Technical Paper A84-26552 11-03, pp. 14-19

HIGGINS, M.W 'Factors and trade-offs affecting ram-air parachutes designed for civilian personnel applications', 6th Aerodynamic Decelerator and Balloon Technology Conference, Houston, Texas, USA, March 1979; New York AIAA 1979; Technical Paper A79-26626 10-01 pp. 250–60

HOBBS, S.E 'A quantitative study of kite performance in natural wind with application to kite anemometry', Phd Thesis, Cranfield Institute of Technology, England, 1986

LEIBECK, R.H 'A class of airfoils designed for high lift in incompressible flow', *Journal of Aircraft*, October 1973, Vol 10, pp. 610–17

LEIBECK, R.H 'Optimization of airfoils for maximum lift', *Journal of Aircraft*, Vol 7(5), Sept. 1970 pp. 409–15

LINGARD, J.S 'The performance and design of ram-air gliding parachutes', *RAE Technical Report* TR81103, 1981

LINGARD, J.S 'The aerodynamics of gliding parachutes'; 'Aerodynamics at low Reynolds numbers: Re greater than 10,000 and less than 1,000,000', International Conference, London, October 1986; *London Aeronautical Society*, Vol 3, 1986, pp. 26·1–26·41

LISSAMAN, P.B 'Low Reynolds number Airfoils', *Annual Review of Fluid Mechanics*, 1983, Vol 15, pp. 223–39

LISSAMAN, P.B 'Design of subsonic airfoils for high lift', *Journal of Aircraft*, Vol 15, pp. 547–61

LUCKING, P *The Sewing Machine Handbook*, B.T. Batsford, 1985

LYNN, P 'Current trends' *Kiteflier* (newsletter of the Kite Society of Great Britain), September 1990

MCMASTERS, J.H 'Low-speed single-element airfoil synthesis', *Technical Soaring*, Vol 6 (2)

MCMASTERS, J.H 'Two airfoil sections

designed for low Reynolds number',
Technical Soaring, Vol 6 (4)

NATHE, G.A 'Analysis of the parafoil',
AIAA Student Journal 5 (1), Feb 1967,
pp. 4–9

NICOLAIDES, J.D, SPEELMAN, R.J and
MENARD, G.L 'A review of parafoil
applications', *Journal of Aircraft* Vol 7
(5), Sept–Oct. 1970

POYNTER, D *Parachute Handbook*, Para
Publishing, Santa Barbara, USA, 3rd ed.
1973

PUSKAS, E 'Ram-air parachute design
considerations and applications', 8th
Aerodynamic Decelerator and Balloon
Technology Conference, Hyannis,
Montana, USA, April 1984; New York,
AIAA 1984; Technical Paper 84-0826
pp. 255–9

RIEGELS, F.W *Aerofoil Sections*,
Butterworths, London, 1961

SIMONS, M *Model aircraft aerodynamics*,
Argus Books, (3rd ed.) 1987

'Sutton Flowform' (press release), Strong
Enterprises (undated)

STANDARDS

BS 3870:
Pt 1 Stitches and seams: classification of
    stitch types
Pt 2 Stitches and seams: classification of
    seam types
British Standards Institute, 1982

PATENTS

Cleveland, C	US 3276730: tail-less kite
Ferrari, P	US D273211: kite
Gargano, G	US 4705238: ram-air parachute with multiple pressure centres
Grauel, E	US 3740008: multi-keeled kite
Hartig, A	US 3347500: kite
Jalbert, D	US 3285546 (re-issued as 26,427): multi-cell wing-type aerial device
Jalbert, D	US 3749337: aerial sled
Puskas, E	GB 2141079: canopy-loading system for ram-air parachutes
Reuter, J.D	US 3524613: flexible gliding wing
Synder, S	US 3724789:parachute
Sutton, S.J	US 3822844: parachute
Sutton, S.J	US 3893641: flowform device

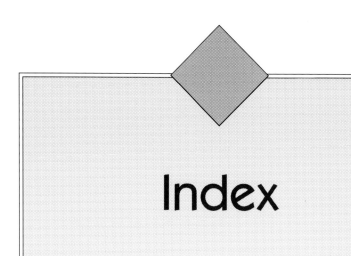

Index